ROYAL TROON
GOLF CLUB

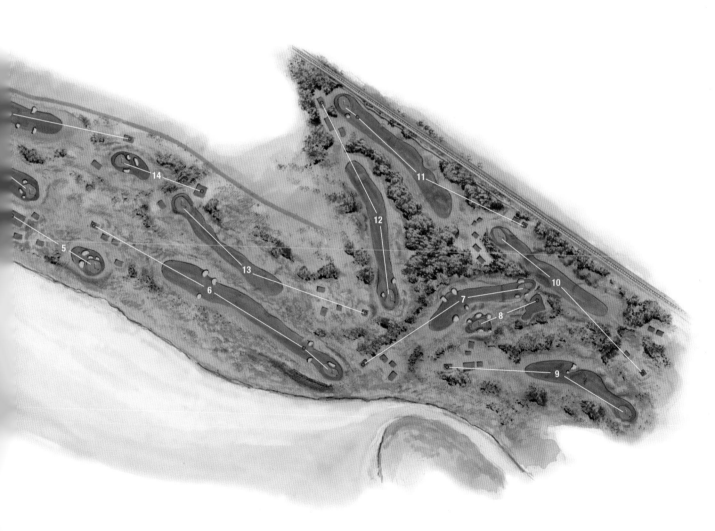

Hazleton Publishing Ltd
5th Floor, Mermaid House, 2 Puddle Dock, London EC4V 3DS
Hazleton Publishing Ltd is a member of Profile Media Group Plc

Published 2004 by Hazleton Publishing Ltd

Copyright © 2004 R&A Championships Limited

Statistics of The 133rd Open Championship produced on a
Unisys Computer System

Course map courtesy of The Majors of Golf

Assistance with records provided by Peter Lewis, Fiona McDougall,
Stewart McDougall and Salvatore Johnson

A CIP catalogue record for this book is available
from the British Library

ISBN: 1-903135-38-9

Design and production by Davis Design
Printed in Great Britain

WRITERS
Robert Sommers

Mike Aitken

Andy Farrell

John Hopkins

Lewine Mair

Michael McDonnell

PHOTOGRAPHERS
Getty Images

David Cannon

Stuart Franklin

Christopher Furlong

Ross Kinnaird

Warren Little

Andrew Redington

Richard Martin-Roberts
Golf Editor

Ian Walton
Chief Technician

EDITOR
Bev Norwood

The Championship Committee

CHAIRMAN
David Pepper

DEPUTY CHAIRMAN
Martin Kippax

COMMITTEE
Geoffrey Clay
John Crawshaw
Charles Donald
Lout Mangelaar Meertens
Richard Muckart
Dougal Rae
Colin Strachan
Peter Unsworth
Martin Yates

ADVISORY MEMBER
William Black
Council of National Golf Unions

CHIEF EXECUTIVE
Peter Dawson

DIRECTOR OF CHAMPIONSHIPS
David Hill

**DIRECTOR OF RULES
AND EQUIPMENT STANDARDS**
David Rickman

Introduction

By David Pepper
Chairman of Championship Committee
The R&A

This year the quest for places in the starting field of 156 players began early. January saw the start of our new International Final Qualifying events in Africa and Australasia, followed by Asia in March, and completed in late June in America and Europe. These groundbreaking events proved to be popular with some 350 world-ranked players who took advantage of this opportunity.

Favourable weather in the early summer enabled Billy McClachlan and his team to bring the condition of the course at Royal Troon up to its peak with its fast-running fairways and smooth greens. The golf course was much praised by the players, who also appreciated both the way in which the course had been set up and the much improved pace of play.

On an exciting final day with many chip shots and long putts being holed, Todd Hamilton bravely retained his lead to the end and held his nerve to triumph over Ernie Els at the final hole in the playoff with a most exquisite run-up stroke from 30 yards.

The Championship Committee are most grateful to the members of Royal Troon Golf Club for the loan of their superb links course and their enthusiastic assistance in running the Championship. Similarly we are indebted to the hundreds of volunteers who helped in so many ways to make the qualifying events as well as the Championship such a success.

Finally I would like to thank the journalists and photographers for their contribution to making this book such a memorable record.

David Pepper

Foreword

By Todd Hamilton

I was fortunate to be the one holding the trophy at the conclusion of The 133rd Open Championship. It could have been any one of four or five players, especially Ernie Els, who played like the champion that he is.

Through the week I was calm, the same feeling I had when I won my first tournament in America earlier in the year. Holding the lead going to the final round, I had never been in a position like that, at least not in a tournament as grand as this, but oddly I was relaxed and the day seemed like fun to me.

I enjoy the style of golf on the links, where you can play the bump-and-run shots onto the greens. Ugly golf, that's what I call it, and I'm usually pretty good at ugly golf, unfortunately. I don't hit the ball as well as a lot of players, but I do have a good short game that allows me to at least be competitive. I keep the ball in play and rely on my chipping and putting.

Much was said and written from Royal Troon about my background in professional golf and the years I spent playing in Asia and Japan. I'm a strong believer that if you can win a tournament, whatever it might be, you can focus on that positive and transfer it to your next match. I had won tournaments before, but nothing on a stage like this. I was trying to look around as much as I could, to soak it all in. To be The Open champion is very special.

Todd Hamilton

The Wethered Principle

By Michael McDonnell

Champions at Royal Troon have demonstrated a common strategy, best defined by Joyce Wethered, later Lady Heathcoat Amory, of focusing solely on the challenges of the golf course, and not on their fellow competitors.

When the distinguished author Henry Leach outlined the charm and challenge of Troon—as it then was in 1907—he wrote that its enduring appeal was to "players who like risks and the overcoming of them." They like "to be called upon to take their lives in their hands at every stroke of their play. This is great golf." It is also the definitive setting for a championship of the highest quality, particularly when such a landscape stretches along the shores of the Firth of Clyde and is subject to the cruel and capricious vagaries of climate that can change fortunes in an instant, underlining the

The par-5 fourth hole, left, provides the best birdie opportunity on the outward nine. The eighth hole, or Postage Stamp (preceding spread), is Royal Troon's most famous.

eternal truth that golf was never meant to be a fair game.

The venerable Gene Sarazen bore sad witness to that maxim when he attempted to qualify for his first Open back in 1923. He took on the nearby Portland links in gale-force conditions and was blown to an 83, yet still held hopes that he might squeeze into the main championship on the basis that others would score badly too. Not so. The wind dropped suddenly in the afternoon, and the courtly American was left with nothing to do but consider his homeward travel plans while others contested the Championship.

Even so, Sarazen declared at the time, "I'll be back, even if I have to swim across." He settled his personal score with The Open by winning in 1932 at Prince's in Kent, and with Troon itself when he was invited back at the age of 71 for the 1973 Championship. He scored a hole-in-one at the 123-yard Postage Stamp eighth hole, to the delight of spectators and television viewers who witnessed the feat.

Moreover, Sarazen scored a birdie 2 at this most feared hole the next day and quipped afterwards,

The tee shot on the par-3 fifth must find the heart of the green because the ground slopes sharply right.

1993 Sandwich

Peter Corrigan
The Independent on Sunday

"Greg Norman's flourish of a final round of 64 was the finest Open climax I have witnessed. Apart from being the lowest last round by any Open winner, it was all the more impressive because baying at his heels were a pack that made up one of the highest quality leaderboards any major championship has seen."

"My putter let me know it was very disturbed at not having been used and it hasn't sunk a putt for me since."

Any study of the champions of Royal Troon down through the years, and in particular the manner in which they triumphed, reveals a common strategy by which they ignored the menace—imagined or real—of their fellow competitors and focused solely on answering and indeed conquering the challenges that the course itself presented.

This attitude was best defined by Lady Heathcoat Amory, who as Joyce Wethered was regarded by Bobby Jones and Henry Cotton as one of the finest strikers in golf. She won the 1925 Ladies British Amateur Championship over the Ayrshire links in a thrilling final against Cecil Leitch, an occasion for which the local dockyard workers were given a half-day holiday so they could take their families to watch these famous golfers in action.

She wrote in 1934, "The game must be played against no particular opponent, but with the sole idea of producing the right figures. If I could only bring myself to forget the excitement and importance of the match I was playing in, then I gave myself an infinitely better chance of reproducing my best form."

She was, of course, referring to match-play golf, but the principle still applies to the card-and-pencil variety because there have been some forlorn victims at Royal Troon who allowed the magnitude of the moment to sabotage their chances of victory. None more so than Bobby Clampett, who was the runaway leader by five strokes after two rounds in the 1982 Championship when an interviewer asked him, "What do you do for the next two rounds, Bobby? Attack or play safe?"

Whether that question preyed on his mind for the remainder of the Championship is not known, but it is a matter of record that he scored 78-77 and finished well down the field. In that same event Nick Price was three strokes clear with four holes to play and, as he said later, "had one hand on the trophy" until he committed a series of blunders that allowed the menacing Tom Watson to become champion and, at the time, only the fifth man in history to have won both the US and British titles in the same year.

More evidence of the Wethered principle—or rather a failure to observe it—was produced by Greg Norman in a playoff for the 1989 title against eventual champion Mark Calcavecchia and Wayne Grady. Norman sought to protect an early lead with a chip shot that did not come off, and then drove into a bunker on the last hole and put his recovery shot out of bounds. He trooped sadly away as yet another chance of success eluded him.

It is this insidious awareness of what is at stake that suddenly intrudes and foils all ability to function with the same excellence that brought the player to the threshold of winning. What is required is

The treacherous 11th hole is also known for the nearby railway line.

The 13th hole marks the start of one of the most difficult finishing stretches in Open Championship golf.

an awareness of the dangers as well as the strength of mind to ignore them, as Tom Weiskopf did in winning the 1973 Open at Troon.

Weiskopf received some invaluable advice from two experienced champions before his final round when he was being challenged by Johnny Miller, who had won the US Open a few weeks earlier and was clearly playing confidently enough to add the British title to his credit. Weiskopf had dinner with Jack Nicklaus on the eve of the final round, and Nicklaus told him, "Don't play Miller tomorrow. Play the course." The Wethered principle again.

On the morning of the final round, Weiskopf received a telephone call from Tony Jacklin, who told him much the same thing. "Lad, if you keep your concentration and play your own game, you will win the greatest of all championships," Jacklin said.

It was an act of thoughtful reciprocation towards his American friend who, before the final round of the 1970 US Open, had left a note, bearing the word "Tempo," in Jacklin's locker. That message had sustained him through the day, and he became the first Englishman in 50 years to win the US title and, indeed, was still holding the British title from the previous year.

Now the favour—if such it was—had been returned and worked to perfection as Weiskopf kept his volatile temperament under control and held off the challenge of Miller to become champion. The poignant aspect of his victory was that his father, who had never doubted that his son would one day become a major winner despite a succession of near-misses, died three months before that great moment.

It is fair to say that Arnold Palmer's defence of his title in 1962, on hard, fast-running fairways, was also a masterpiece of skill and control as he throttled back on his enormous power to keep the

Round Royal Troon

No 1 • 370 yards Par 4
What was once a gentle introduction has been toughened by moving the tee right towards the beach, with two new bunkers on the right of the fairway. While the hole has been lengthened by only six yards from 1997, getting home in two is no longer a formality.

No 2 • 391 yards Par 4
Three cross-bunkers within range from the tee dictate strategy, particularly downwind, and the preferred procedure is to play short to take them out of play for an approach to the pear-shaped green protected by another three bunkers at the front.

No 3 • 379 yards Par 4
The Gyaws Burn crosses the fairway some 300 yards from the tee. The wise precaution to avert a possible crisis so early in the round is to lay up for a less hazardous approach to a green with two bunkers to the left and one to the right.

No 4 • 560 yards Par 5
An extra three yards have been added since 1997, when it was rated as the easiest hole, with 20 eagles recorded, but the addition of two bunkers to the left of the fairway now limit the freedom of the big hitters to attack with confidence.

No 5 • 210 yards Par 3
The tee shot must find the heart of the green irrespective of the pin position, because the ground drops sharply to the right towards the shore and deep bunkers protect the front of this large green.

No 6 • 601 yards Par 5
Already the longest hole in Open Championship golf, it has been lengthened by 24 yards from 1997. The power players can still reach the green in two, but for lesser mortals the wise route is to play short of the left-hand greenside bunkers then pitch on.

No 7 • 405 yards Par 4
Another three yards have been added since the last Open, laying great emphasis on accuracy from an elevated tee to a narrow landing area flanked by bunkers left and right, and then to a heavily bunkered green set steeply in the dunes.

No 8 • 123 yards Par 3
No need to alter a masterpiece. This is the shortest hole on The Open roster but amongst the most feared. Cavernous bunkers on all sides dictate that the only safe error is to over-hit the green for a simple chip shot back.

No 9 • 423 yards Par 4
One of the most difficult outward holes and capable of seriously damaging a potentially good score. Accordingly, it must be treated with respect, with a tee shot short of the left-hand bunkers for a demanding approach through a narrow gully to a two-tiered green.

No 10 • 438 yards Par 4
Even without intervening bunkers, this is still an extremely demanding hole. The blind tee shot is followed by an approach to a green which falls away sharply to the right, and is therefore a most elusive target.

No 11 • 490 yards Par 4
Lengthened by 27 yards, it remains a daunting challenge as a two-shotter with gorse bushes both sides of the fairway, which falls to the right and towards the out-of-bounds stone wall and railway line beside the green.

No 12 • 431 yards Par 4
A narrow two-tiered green makes the pin extremely difficult to attack. The correct angle of approach is essential and thereby places subtle emphasis on what seems an undemanding tee shot to a fairway that curves towards the right.

No 13 • 472 yards Par 4
A modest addition of seven yards on this hole which heralds the start of what some consider the most difficult finishing stretch in Open Championship golf. Two powerful strokes are required to reach the elevated green along a fairway that does not need the menace of bunkers to add to its challenge.

No 14 • 178 yards Par 3
The wise strategy on this apparently simple hole is to play the tee shot long to avoid the three protective front bunkers, and thereby find the wide area of the green and allow the putter to tidy up for a birdie or par.

No 15 • 483 yards Par 4
A new tee has been constructed, adding 26 yards to the hole since 1997, but it still requires a long straight drive between fairway bunkers so that the second shot can be threaded carefully to a well-protected, sunken green.

No 16 • 542 yards Par 5
A crucial decision awaits late in the round for the big hitters on whether to carry the ditch which crosses the fairway for a simple and direct route to the green. A new bunker on the left side, just beyond the ditch, increases the need for precision as well as power.

No 17 • 222 yards Par 3
The third most difficult hole in the 1997 Championship. The vagaries of weather can dictate anything from a driver to a long iron from the tee to a green that falls away on both sides and is difficult to hold in the prevailing wind from the left.

No 18 • 457 yards Par 4
An inhospitable conclusion with the carry to the fairway of around 225 yards to a landing area menaced by three bunkers to the left and one to the right. Another bunker lies in wait to protect the final green, at the back of which is a path and out of bounds.

It is best to play the tee shot long on the par-3 14th hole to avoid the three protective bunkers.

ball in play and away from the terrors that lurked so close to the undulating fairways and seemed to ambush the rest of the field, leaving Arnie in splendid isolation at the top of the leaderboard.

Before the Championship, Palmer analysed and pinpointed the specific danger areas at Troon and formulated his plans accordingly. The late Pat Ward-Thomas wrote a compelling account for *Country Life* a week after the Championship and observed, "Palmer said that the 11th would be the key hole. It was difficult, dangerous, and greatly dependent on the bounce of the ball.

"The tee shot had to be played on a line crossing the fairway towards thick gorse on the left, with rough and gorse on the right as well. An unkind kick could mean any number of strokes. Even if the tee shot was safely contrived, the long second to an uphill green, hard against the railway wall, was fearsome indeed.

"In five rounds, including the qualifying, Palmer had two 3s, two 4s, and an unlucky 5 when his ball finished inches through the green in thick grass. Never will I forget the sight of Palmer's rifling sec-ond shots, with a one or two iron, that subdued the hole as no one else in the world could have done."

Essentially, Palmer had blocked the rest of the field from his thoughts in order to produce his best golf, and said as much in his 1964 book *Portrait of a Professional Golfer*. "I don't think I fear opponents," Palmer wrote. "But I do respect them and what they can do. There's a difference. Fear makes people jittery, but sensible respect balances things out—puts them in their proper perspective."

It says much for his fortitude that he was able to regain his competitive confidence only a few weeks after losing the US Open in a playoff to then-newcomer Jack Nicklaus. Troon was to be a cultural shock for the Golden Bear, who still had much to learn about seaside golf and finished down amongst the supporting cast, some 29 strokes behind the winner.

What sets Royal Troon apart as a championship test is that the examination it presents is both exhaustive and relentless in that each stroke—even a good one—can prompt a subsequent problem.

Exempt Competitors

Name, Country	Category
Robert Allenby, Australia	3, 17
Stephen Ames, Canada	3
Stuart Appleby, Australia	3, 13, 17
Arjun Atwal, India	18
Rich Beem, USA	13
Thomas Bjorn, Denmark	1, 3
Mark Calcavecchia, USA	2
Chad Campbell, USA	3, 13
Michael Campbell, New Zealand	4
Paul Casey, England	3, 4
Dinesh Chand, Fiji	25
K J Choi, Korea	3, 17
Stewart Cink, USA	3
Tim Clark, South Africa	17
Darren Clarke, N. Ireland	3, 4
Ben Curtis, USA	1, 2, 3
John Daly, USA	2
Brian Davis, England	1, 4
Chris DiMarco, USA	3, 13
Scott Drummond, Scotland	5
Ernie Els, South Africa	2, 3, 4, 13, 17
Gary Evans, England	1
Nick Faldo, England	1, 2
Brad Faxon, USA	3, 13
Darren Fichardt, South Africa	20
*Nick Flanagan, Australia	28
Steve Flesch, USA	3
Alastair Forsyth, Scotland	4
Keiichiro Fukabori, Japan	22
Jim Furyk, USA	3, 9, 13, 17
Sergio Garcia, Spain	1, 3
Ignacio Garrido, Spain	4, 5
Retief Goosen, South Africa	1, 3, 9, 17
Richard Green, Australia	7
Jay Haas, USA	3, 5, 13, 17
Joakim Haeggman, Sweden	6
Todd Hamilton, USA	3, 23
Anders Hansen, Denmark	5
Padraig Harrington, Ireland	3, 4
Tetsuji Hiratsuka, Japan	23
S K Ho, Korea	25
Hidemasa Hoshino, Japan	25
Charles Howell III, USA	3, 13, 17
David Howell, England	4
John Huston, USA	3
Trevor Immelman, South Africa	3, 4

Name, Country	Category
Fredrik Jacobson, Sweden	1, 3, 4
Raphael Jacquelin, France	4
Miguel Angel Jimenez, Spain	3
Zach Johnson, USA	3
Brendan Jones, Australia	24
Takashi Kamiyama, Japan	25
Jonathan Kaye, USA	3, 13
Jerry Kelly, USA	3, 17
Barry Lane, England	6
Paul Lawrie, Scotland	2
Stephen Leaney, Australia	3, 4, 17
Tom Lehman, USA	2
Justin Leonard, USA	2, 3, 13, 17
Thomas Levet, France	8
Frank Lickliter, USA	15
Peter Lonard, Australia	3, 4, 17, 19
Davis Love III, USA	1, 3, 12, 13, 17
Steve Lowery, USA	16
Sandy Lyle, Scotland	2
Shigeki Maruyama, Japan	3
Graeme McDowell, N. Ireland	6
*Brian McElhinney, Ireland	29

Scoring in Opens at Troon

Lowest Aggregate
272 (69, 66, 72, 65), Justin Leonard, 1997

Lowest Round
64, Greg Norman, fourth round, 1989;
Tiger Woods, third round, 1997

Lowest First Round
66, Wayne Stephens, 1989;
Paul Casey, Thomas Levet, 2004

Lowest Second Round
65, Payne Stewart, 1989

Lowest Third Round
64, Tiger Woods, 1997

Lowest Fourth Round
64, Greg Norman, 1989

Name, Country	Category	Name, Country	Category
Shaun Micheel, USA	3, 11	Chris Riley, USA	3
Phil Mickelson, USA	3, 10, 17	Rory Sabbatini, South Africa	15
Greg Norman, Australia	2	Adam Scott, Australia	3, 4
Peter O'Malley, Australia	8	Vijay Singh, Fiji	1, 3, 10, 13, 17
Mark O'Meara, USA	2	David Toms, USA	3, 11, 13, 17
Hennie Otto, South Africa	1	Bob Tway, USA	3, 13, 21
Craig Parry, Australia	3	Scott Verplank, USA	3, 13
Craig Perks, New Zealand	12	Mike Weir, Canada	3, 10, 13, 17
Kenny Perry, USA	1, 3, 13, 17	Tom Weiskopf, USA	2
Ian Poulter, England	3, 4	Lee Westwood, England	4
Nick Price, Zimbabwe	2, 3, 13, 17	*Stuart Wilson, Scotland	27
Phillip Price, Wales	1, 4	Tiger Woods, USA	1, 2, 3, 9, 10, 11, 13, 17
Jean Francois Remesy, France	7		

* Denotes amateurs

Key to Exemptions from Regional, Local Final and International Final Qualifying

Exemptions for 2004 were granted to the following:

(1) First 10 and anyone tying for 10th place in the 2003 Open Championship.

(2) Past Open Champions aged 65 or under on 18 July 2004.

(3) The first 50 players on the Official World Golf Ranking as at 27 May 2004.

(4) First 20 in the PGA European Tour Final Volvo Order of Merit for 2003.

(5) The Volvo PGA Champions for 2002-2004.

(6) First 3 and anyone tying for 3rd place, not otherwise exempt, in the top 20 of the PGA European Tour Volvo Order of Merit for 2004 at 27 May 2004.

(7) First 2 European Tour members and any European Tour members tying for 2nd place, not otherwise exempt, in a cumulative money list taken from all official PGA European Tour events from the Deutsche Bank – SAP Open TPC of Europe up to and including the Smurfit European Open and including The US Open.

(8) The leading player, not otherwise exempt having applied (7) above, in each of the 2004 Smurfit European Open and the 2004 Barclays Scottish Open. Ties will be decided by the better final round score and, if still tied, by the better third round score and then by the better second round score. If still tied, all players thus tying will be deemed exempt under this category.

(9) The US Open Champions for 2000-2004.

(10) The US Masters Champions for 2000-2004.

(11) The USPGA Champions for 1999-2003.

(12) The USPGA Tour Players Champions for 2002-2004.

(13) First 20 on the Official Money List of the USPGA Tour for 2003.

(14) First 3 and anyone tying for 3rd place, not otherwise exempt, in the top 20 of the Official Money List of the USPGA Tour for 2004 at 27 May 2004.

(15) First 2 USPGA Tour members and any USPGA Tour members tying for 2nd place, not otherwise exempt, in a cumulative money list taken from the USPGA Tour Players Championship and the 5 USPGA Tour events leading up to and including the 2004 Western Open.

(16) The leading player, not otherwise exempt having applied (15) above, in each of the 2004 Western Open and the 2004 John Deere Classic. Ties will be decided by the better final round score and, if still tied, by the better third round score and then by the better second round score. If still tied, all players thus still tying will be deemed exempt under this category.

(17) Playing members of the 2003 Presidents Cup teams.

(18) First and anyone tying for 1st place on the Order of Merit of the Asian PGA Tour for 2003.

(19) First 2 and anyone tying for 2nd place on the Order of Merit of the Tour of Australasia for 2003.

(20) First and anyone tying for 1st place on the Order of Merit of the Southern Africa PGA Sunshine Tour for 2003/2004.

(21) The Canadian Open Champion for 2003.

(22) The Japan Open Champion for 2003.

(23) First 3 and anyone tying for 3rd place on the Japan Golf Tour for 2003.

(24) The leading player, not otherwise exempt, in the 2004 Mizuno Open.

(25) First 4 and anyone tying for 4th place, not otherwise exempt having applied (24) above, in the top 20 of a cumulative money list taken from all official Japan Golf Tour events from the 2004 Japan PGA Championship up to and including the 2004 Mizuno Open.

(26) The Senior British Open Champion for 2003.

(27) The Amateur Champion for 2004.

(28) The US Amateur Champion for 2003.

(29) The European Individual Amateur Champion for 2003.

Note: Exemption for performance as an amateur under (27) to (29) would only be granted if the entrant concerned was still an amateur on 15 July 2004.

Local Final Qualifying
10-11 July

Glasgow (Gailes)

Simon Dyson, England, 65-72–137
Paul Bradshaw, England, 71-70–141
Andrew Willey, England, 68-73–141
(P)Anthony Millar, England, 70-72–142
(R)Brett Taylor, England, 73-69–142

Irvine

Jonathan Cheetham, England, 66-68–134
Martin Erlandsson, Sweden, 68-67–135
(P)Sven Struver, Germany, 69-70–139
(P)Andrew Oldcorn, Scotland, 66-73–139
(R)Ian Spencer, England, 69-70–139

Turnberry Kintyre

Paul Wesselingh, England, 68-69–137
Sean Whiffin, England, 67-70–137
*Steven Tiley, England, 67-70–137
*Lloyd Campbell, England, 67-70–137
(R)Neil Evans, England, 70-68–138

Western Gailes

Daniel Sugrue, Ireland, 67-72–139
Ben Willman, England, 67-74–141
(P)Lewis Atkinson, England, 70-72–142
(R)Barry Hume, Scotland, 71-71–142
(R)David Griffiths, England, 72-71–143

* Denotes amateurs   (P) Qualified after playoff
(R) Qualified as a reserve

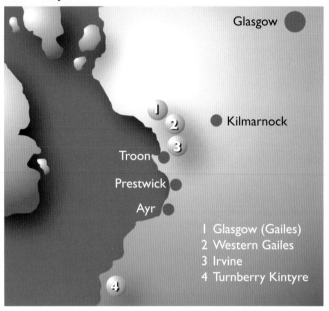

Reserve No 1 Barry Hume (Western Gailes) qualified when Mark Hensby (John Deere Classic) did not take up the place (qualification 16) for "the leading player, not otherwise exempt..."

Reserve No 2 Ian Spencer (Irvine) qualified when Toshi Izawa (Exempt Competitor) withdrew because of a severe sinus infection.

Reserve No 3 Neil Evans (Turnberry Kintyre) qualified when Warren Bennett (International Final Qualifying in Europe) withdrew because of a shoulder injury.

Reserve No 4 Brett Taylor (Glasgow Gailes) qualified when Andre Stolz (Exempt Competitor) withdrew with no reason given.

Reserve No 5 David Griffiths (Western Gailes) qualified when David Duval (Exempt Competitor) withdrew because of a strained back muscle.

International Final Qualifying

ASIA 30-31 March
Saujana — *Kuala Lumpur, Malaysia*

Scott Barr, Australia	67	72	139
Kim Felton, Australia	70	69	139
Jyoti Randhawa, India	71	68	139
Yoshinobu Tsukada, Japan	69	71	140

Jyoti Randhawa

AMERICA 28 June
Congressional — *Bethesda, Maryland*

Carl Pettersson, Sweden	71	63	134
Mathias Gronberg, Sweden	69	65	134
Spike McRoy, USA	69	65	134
Bo Van Pelt, USA	69	66	135
Mathew Goggin, Australia	68	67	135
Steve Elkington, Australia	69	66	135
Rodney Pampling, Australia	66	69	135
Tim Herron, USA	69	67	136
Hunter Mahan, USA	64	72	136
Luke Donald, England	70	67	137
Skip Kendall, USA	65	72	137
Bob Estes, USA	68	69	137
Aaron Baddeley, Australia	69	68	137
Glen Day, USA	70	67	137
Cameron Beckman, USA	71	66	137

Carl Pettersson

AUSTRALASIA 19-20 January
Kingston Heath — *Melbourne, Australia*

Andrew Buckle, Australia	71	67	138
Adam Le Vesconte, Australia	69	69	138
Matthew Hazelden, England	73	68	141
Brendan Jones, Australia	69	72	141

Adam Le Vesconte

Royal Troon ★

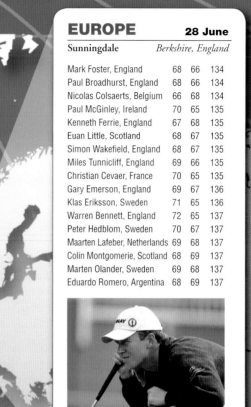

EUROPE   28 June
Sunningdale   *Berkshire, England*

Mark Foster, England	68	66	134
Paul Broadhurst, England	68	66	134
Nicolas Colsaerts, Belgium	66	68	134
Paul McGinley, Ireland	70	65	135
Kenneth Ferrie, England	67	68	135
Euan Little, Scotland	68	67	135
Simon Wakefield, England	68	67	135
Miles Tunnicliff, England	69	66	135
Christian Cevaer, France	70	65	135
Gary Emerson, England	69	67	136
Klas Eriksson, Sweden	71	65	136
Warren Bennett, England	72	65	137
Peter Hedblom, Sweden	70	67	137
Maarten Lafeber, Netherlands	69	68	137
Colin Montgomerie, Scotland	68	69	137
Marten Olander, Sweden	69	68	137
Eduardo Romero, Argentina	68	69	137

Mark Foster

AFRICA   8-9 January
Atlantic Beach   *Cape Town, South Africa*

James Kingston, South Africa	66	69	135
Louis Oosthuizen, South Africa	66	72	138
Tjaart van der Walt, South Africa	67	71	138
Grant Muller, South Africa		69	71	140

James Kingston

Balls Flying Into The Holes

By Robert Sommers

There was even an albatross in the first round and Royal Troon's par of 71 was broken by 39 players as England's Paul Casey and France's Thomas Levet shared the lead at 66, three strokes ahead of the home favourite, Colin Montgomerie.

Two years before the start of The Open Championship, Gary Evans's golf ball had disappeared in the heavy grass alongside Muirfield's 17th hole during the final round of the 2002 Championship. Here at Royal Troon, once again he had a ball disappear on him, this time on the fourth hole. The first had cost him two strokes and possibly the 2002 Championship, since he had missed a place in the playoff by a stroke.

At Royal Troon, though, his ball had vanished because he had holed a 227-yard five iron and scored an albatross 2, or three under par, on the 560-yard fourth hole.

After an ace at the eighth, Ernie Els took double bogey at 17.

His had been an unusual shot, to be sure, but, on this day, hardly unique. For a time at least, it seemed that balls were flying into the holes with alarming frequency. To wit:

Kenny Perry holed a 70-yard pitch and eagled the first.

K J Choi ripped a 235-yard five iron onto the fourth green and eagled with a three-foot putt.

Rich Beem, who had been out of the limelight since he won the 2002 USPGA Championship, reached the 601-yard sixth with a three wood for his second and holed from four feet for an eagle.

And before most of the gallery had wiped the sleep from their eyes, Ernie Els pitched a sand wedge onto the eighth green, the 123-yard Postage Stamp, and watched the ball bounce twice, then draw back into the cup for a hole-in-one.

Spectacular shots claimed their toll, for this had been a tough day on Royal Troon. The old course that sits alongside the Firth of Clyde surrendered 10 eagles plus Evans's albatross, the eagles divided equally between the fourth and the sixth holes, the longest on The Open's rota of courses, and at the same time gave up 410 birdies.

1

Excerpts FROM THE Press

Thursday Weather
Fair with a southwesterly breeze.

WELCOME TO ROYAL TROON

Of the 156 men who played Royal Troon that day, the elite of the game, 39 men broke its demanding par of 71, a quarter of the field, and 17 others matched it. The field averaged 72.91 strokes.

By day's end, 25 men had turned in scores in the 60s. Some of their appetites for birdies approached the gluttonous.

Paul Casey, a 26-year-old Englishman, birdied seven holes and tied Frenchman Thomas Levet for first place with 66. Levet, Barry Lane, Shaun Micheel, the 2003 USPGA champion, Christian Cevaer, and Lee Westwood each birdied six holes, and 15 others birdied five, among them Thomas Bjorn, who nevertheless shot 74. After nearly winning at Sandwich a year earlier, Bjorn also parred just six holes, bogeyed six, and dropped two strokes on the par-4 11th.

Among the leaders, Michael Campbell of New Zealand returned a 67 and nine others tied at 68, a group that included Vijay Singh, Choi, Evans, on the wings of his albatross, Englishman Kenneth Ferrie, and two Scots, Alastair Forsyth and Stuart Wilson, the Amateur champion. Bogeys on the treacherous 17th set back both Choi and Evans and, in position to share first place, Forsyth lost strokes on both the closing holes.

Forsyth had played in his first Open at Sandwich a year earlier and survived the 36-hole cut, and now, at the age of 26, he stood close to leading the field. In the next-to-last group to tee off late in the day, he bumbled his start by dropping a stroke at the first but recovered

Peter O'Malley struck the first tee shot at 6.30 am.

From the left rough on the 11th, Thomas Levet ripped a six-iron shot 200 yards, to 10 feet from the hole for a birdie.

by birdieing the third. His name flashed on the leaderboards when he eagled the sixth and birdied the seventh and eighth, three holes played in eight strokes against a par of 12.

A par on the ninth and Forsyth had played the first nine in 32, four under par. Coming back he lost a stroke at the 12th, but he birdied the 13th and 15th. At five under, he could have caught both Casey and Levet, but lost his chance with the two closing bogeys.

Like Forsyth, Wilson had played in one previous Open, his at Lytham in 2001, where he missed the 36-hole cut. Unless his game collapsed utterly in the second round, he would celebrate his 27th birthday on the links of Royal Troon on Sunday. Here he played the first nine in 32 and came back in 36 for his 68.

With scores of 69, two under par, 13 players shared 13th place, a group that included Els, Perry, Beem, Colin Montgomerie, Darren Clarke, Barry Lane, and Retief Goosen, who had won his second US Open Championship four weeks earlier.

First Round Leaders

HOLE	1	2	3	4	5	6	7	8	9	10	11	12	13	14	15	16	17	18	
PAR	4	4	4	5	3	5	4	3	4	4	4	4	4	3	4	5	3	4	TOTAL
Paul Casey	(3)	4	4	(4)	3	5	4	(2)	[5]	(3)	(3)	[5]	4	3	4	(4)	3	(3)	66
Thomas Levet	4	4	4	(4)	(2)	5	(3)	(2)	4	[5]	(3)	4	4	3	4	5	(2)	4	66
Michael Campbell	4	4	4	(4)	3	(3)	4	3	(3)	[5]	4	4	4	3	(3)	5	3	4	67
Gary Evans	4	4	4	(2)	3	[6]	4	3	4	4	4	(3)	4	3	4	(4)	[4]	4	68
K J Choi	4	4	4	(3)	3	(4)	4	3	4	4	(3)	[6]	(3)	3	(3)	5	[4]	4	68
Carl Pettersson	(3)	(3)	(3)	5	3	5	4	3	4	4	[5]	4	4	3	4	(4)	3	4	68
Mathew Goggin	4	(3)	4	(4)	3	(4)	4	3	[5]	4	4	4	(3)	3	[5]	(4)	3	4	68
Kenneth Ferrie	4	4	(3)	5	3	(4)	(3)	(2)	[5]	4	4	4	[5]	3	4	5	3	(3)	68
*Stuart Wilson	(3)	4	4	(4)	3	(4)	(3)	3	4	4	4	4	4	[4]	4	5	3	4	68
Vijay Singh	4	(3)	(3)	5	[4]	(4)	4	(2)	4	4	[5]	4	4	3	4	(4)	3	4	68
Martin Olander	(3)	4	(3)	5	3	5	(3)	3	4	4	[5]	4	4	3	4	(4)	3	4	68
Alastair Forsyth	[5]	4	(3)	5	3	(3)	(3)	(2)	4	4	4	[5]	(3)	3	(3)	5	[4]	[5]	68

* Denotes amateurs

Both Els and Clarke could have done better, but Els caught a bunker on the 17th, took two strokes to recover, and took a 5, and Clarke mis-clubbed on the 18th and overshot the green. His ball ran onto a gravel path before the clubhouse and beyond the out-of-bounds markers. Two strokes gone, he scored 6.

Despite consecutive bogeys on the 12th and 13th, Tiger Woods had a 70, one under par, a score matched by three other former Open champions—Justin Leonard, who won the last Open at Royal Troon, in 1997, Sandy Lyle, and John Daly.

Nick Price and Mark O'Meara, both former Open champions, matched Royal Troon's par of 71, along with 15 others, probably the most noticeable among them Ian Poulter, although not for his golf game.

Adorned in trousers tailored from the Union Jack, Poulter reminded those with good memories of the comment by a journalist during the 1990 Open as he blanched at American golfer Payne Stewart bedecked in a stars-and-stripes shirt. After a moment's pause while he recovered from the surprise, our friend decided Stewart had "dressed as if for burial at sea."

Ian Poulter said he was honouring Payne Stewart.

The Scots Have A Great Day

By Mike Aitken

While Ian Poulter's spectacular Union Jack trousers were a colourful talking point, the Saltire was also generously represented on the opening day at Royal Troon thanks to some eye-catching golf from the Scottish quartet of Colin Montgomerie, Alastair Forsyth, Stuart Wilson, the Amateur champion, and Sandy Lyle, the 1985 Open champion.

No Scot, of course, felt more at home on the links than Montgomerie. A son of the seaside town and member of the club, Montgomerie made new friends and won admiration from old friends for his wise and witty speech given on the Tuesday night at the annual Association of Golf Writers dinner.

It was common knowledge that Montgomerie had been through trying times since the break-up of his marriage to Eimear earlier in the year. At Troon, though, Monty found the support and the affection of a nation sufficient to put his troubles behind him. He reminded the guests at the AGW function how Royal Troon's Latin

Bogeys here at the 17th and the 18th cost Alastair Forsyth a share of the lead.

motto—*Tam arte quam marte*—"as much by skill as by strength"—was in need of updating. "If you're not three under by the turn," he translated for the benefit of the non-members in the field, "then God help you."

In a compelling opening 69, Monty heeded his own advice. Fortified by a fine outward half, he only lost his way when errors on the 10th and 11th yielded double bogey and bogey to take him back to level par. "What the crowd did on the 12th green,

With a nine-iron shot to the second green and a 20-foot putt, Colin Montgomerie was off with his first birdie.

when I sank that birdie putt, was fantastic," he recalled. "They knew I had dropped three strokes in the previous two holes and their encouragement helped me to break 70. I know I wouldn't have done that otherwise. If what happened at the 10th and 11th had happened two or three months ago, I wouldn't have recovered.

"But I've had fantastic support from people everywhere, not just on the golf course. Playing here at Troon, I was always going to receive more encouragement than I would anywhere else, but this Open could not have come at a better time for me. I don't feel as alone as you might think."

Lyle's name might have been on everyone's lips too, but four bogeys wiped away most of what he achieved with five birdies; although, at 70 with two nines of 35, he was under par as well. At age 46, playing in his 29th Open, Lyle carried slim expectations of being a contender. Nevertheless, his last two effective starts in The Open had been in Scotland, both times at Muirfield, when he returned 68 in the first rounds in 1992 and 2002.

Forsyth, from Paisley, is often billed as one of the Scots best equipped to pick up the torch from Montgomerie. In his second Open, Forsyth carded his lowest Open score of 68 for joint fourth place with eight others including Wilson. Though rarely mentioned in the same breath as Poulter, Paul Casey, and other high-profile Englishmen such as Luke Donald and Justin Rose, Forsyth is just as capable of developing into a top-class player.

"People at home are always asking if it annoys me, but it doesn't," Forsyth, 28 years of age, replied when asked about the attention showered on his English contemporaries. "In the end, it's all to do with profile. I think the difference with the young Scottish guys is they're a bit quieter and are more the types who creep up on you."

Forsyth's first impression was how the lengthening of the Royal Troon links wouldn't suit him. In fact, it could hardly have been more to his liking until a bogey, bogey finish.

Stuart Wilson went out in 32 with four birdies.

Playing with Mark O'Meara and Michael Campbell, Wilson, from Forfar, was grateful for the past Open champion's willingness to put him at ease when his nerves were jangling over the opening holes. By the time Wilson holed a 25-foot putt on the 18th green to save par and post a 68 which put him among the leaders, it was his professional partners who provided the admiring glances.

Playing in his second Open, Wilson reached the turn in 32 before producing a brilliant sequence of recovery shots over the inward half. Perhaps remembering how Barclay Howard won the amateur medal seven years earlier, the crowd gave Wilson the kind of rousing reception reserved for champions when he made that tramline putt on the last.

Wilson was a key member of the Great Britain and Ireland side in 2003 which defeated the US in the Walker Cup at Ganton. Having taken time off his work at Auchterlonie's Golf Shop in Monifeith, the Scottish internationalist spent the week of The Open sleeping in a caravan. Previously an assistant golf professional at Blairgowrie, Wilson was reinstated to the amateur ranks in 1999 when he decided it would be less of a risk if he completed his education rather than try his luck on the professional circuit.

As a result of his sparkling opening round, Wilson would go on to follow in the footsteps of fellow Scots Charlie Green, who took home the Silver Medal for the leading amateur from Troon in 1962, and Howard, who repeated the feat over the Ayrshire links in 1997. Not only that, but the Sunday would be Wilson's 27th birthday.

Sandy Lyle had a 70 despite four bogeys.

In the Words of the Competitors…

"

"When you play well at the start of The Open, your confidence is right there. When you play that well, you don't really feel the pressure, because you know you are going to make things happen. So it's just a question of staying patient and relaxing on the golf course, and basically what I tell myself is to just keep smiling."

—**Thomas Levet**

"My caddie, Andy, and I decided to take it very patiently today, and in the morning the weather was on my side."

—**K J Choi**

"I didn't play like I normally do, but I scored really well."

—**Vijay Singh**

"Jos (Vanstiphout, psychologist) set me down on Tuesday and told me you're wasting your time, you've got to start winning golf tournaments. He changed my whole mindset very, very quickly."

—**Michael Campbell**

"To shoot a good score in any tournament is always pleasing, and to do it in The Open is even better."

—**Kenneth Ferrie**

"

K J Choi's round included an eagle on the fourth and a double bogey on the 12th.

Vijay Singh said he made adjustments for the lack of wind.

After a birdie on the first, Ben Curtis returned a 75.

Key to Michael Campbell's 67 was an eagle at the sixth.

Appropriately, Poulter wore plus-fours the rest of the week, in honour of Stewart, who died in 1999.

And among those who did not play so well, Ben Curtis, the surprise winner at Sandwich a year ago, began defense of his Championship by shooting a dismal 75, just two strokes worse than the 73 posted by Phil Mickelson, winner of the Masters Tournament earlier in 2004.

The weather did not play its usual intrusive role, although the first day seemed cool. As the round opened, a good many players put on their sweaters, for this had not been the same mild and pleasant temperatures as last year at Sandwich. In fact, a spokesman for the Met office described the weather of the previous four or five weeks as "pretty bloody awful," with cold temperatures, overcast skies, and rain.

Dull grey skies had indeed hovered overhead through most of a very long day—the first group opened the Championship at 6.30 in the morning, and the last teed off at 4.21 that afternoon.

Meanwhile, with the Scottish galleries solidly behind him and himself seemingly in a good mood, Montgomerie played only his second opening round in the 60s in this old Championship. He had

Low Scores	
Low First Nine	
Rich Beem	31
Kenny Perry	31
Low Second Nine	
Paul Casey	32
Low Round	
Paul Casey	66
Thomas Levet	66

Players Below Par	39
Players At Par	17
Players Above Par	100

A trail of smoke usually reveals Darren Clarke, who had a 69 after taking 6 on the 18th hole.

1964 St Andrews

Raymond Jacobs
The Herald (retired)

"Tony Lema at St Andrews in 1964. That was the first Open I covered. He had never played links golf, arrived at St Andrews in time to play nine holes of practice, and when Jack Nicklaus had cut his lead to two strokes in the third round, Tony played the seventh through the 11th in level 3s."

scored 65 in the first round at Royal Lytham and St Annes in 2001 and 69 here at Royal Troon.

For a time at least both Rich Beem and, later in the day, Kenny Perry looked as if they might charge to the front. Both men played Royal Troon's first nine in 31 strokes, but both fizzled with 38s coming in.

Speaking of the inward holes, Perry said, "It's very difficult, two totally different nines. You have the wind helping you going out, then left-to-right coming in.

"It was disappointing to end that way, but all-in-all, I'm tickled. Any time you shoot under par in any round of The Open Championship, you've played well."

While Perry and most of the others in this superb field followed custom in making their birdies early, Casey rushed to the front by wrenching four birdies from the second nine and dropping just one stroke on the stingy 12th, which yielded just nine birdies all day. That had been his second lost stroke, but his seven birdies helped soothe the pain.

A year earlier, playing in his second Open, Casey had opened with

Out in 31 strokes, Kenny Perry posted a 69 with three bogeys on the inward nine.

The man with the albatross, Gary Evans was three under after the fourth.

"The bunkers at Royal Troon are so deep, legend has it one of them became the home address of a refugee caddie during the Second World War. Certainly, Ernie Els must have felt like crawling into the steep-faced hazard that guards the 17th green."

—**Derek Lawrenson**, *Daily Mail*

"No wind to speak of and no-names high on the leaderboard. But so, too, did the first round of The Open at Royal Troon have no shortage of dramatic shots."

—**Jim McCabe**, *Boston Globe*

"Paul Lawrie almost hit an ice cream van at Troon—but Sandy Lyle might just have the course licked. Scotland's former Open champions suffered a day of contrasting fortunes."

—**Gary Ralston**, *Daily Record*

"Kenny Perry played Royal Troon as it was designed. He made his mark on the more docile outward nine, then hung on for dear life coming home."

—**Helen Ross**, *PGATOUR.com*

"A shot which he hoped would take him into a share of The Open Championship lead left Darren Clarke looking stunned yesterday. His five iron from 191 yards ran over the green and up onto the out-of-bounds path in front of the clubhouse."

—**Mark Garrod**, *The Herald*

It Could Be Better (Or Worse)

The pleasure of one helped Ernie Els cleanse his mind of the other

It took 1 on the eighth hole ...

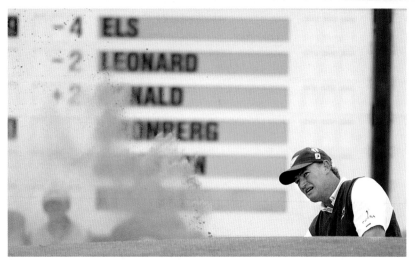

... and 5 on the 17th hole for Ernie Els's 69.

It is not often a player aces one par-3 and takes a 5 on another. Not in the same round at least. When Ernie Els looked back on his day's work, he could conclude that while his opening round of 69, two under par, could have been better, it wasn't a bad start to The Open Championship. He had not done his status as a pre-tournament favourite any harm. "Anything under 70 in a major championship is a pretty good score," Els said.

Els's smile was as wide as the African continent when the ball he had hit with a pitching wedge took two bounces and popped into the hole on the Postage Stamp, the par-3 eighth hole, but not half so wide after he had taken two strokes to get out of the second bunker on the left approaching the 17th green. There was symmetry in that these occurrences happened on the penultimate hole on the outward nine and the penultimate hole on the inward nine. The pleasure of one helped cleanse the mind of the other.

It was the seventh ace of Els's professional career, his second in a major championship, and a rash of holed strokes on the first day was a foretaste of things to come. It was a treat for everyone to see so many shots being made from off the putting surfaces of so many different holes, especially, as it was, in a major championship.

Els might well say that were he to play the 17th again he would not make the same mistake as he did on the first day. His tee shot did not move to the right on the wind as he had expected. That was so small a failure it hardly can be classified as a mistake, not on a 222-yard hole ranked on the day as the seventh most difficult, where the average score was 3.22 and four other double bogeys and one higher score were recorded.

His mistake came when he was a little too cavalier with his second shot, his bunker shot, not giving it the attention it deserved. He thinned it slightly, so instead of the ball clearing the face of the bunker, it thudded into it. Els said later that it was nothing like so difficult as the majestic recovery he made from a deep bunker on the left side of the 13th green at Muirfield in the last round of the 2002 Open, which he won.

"It wasn't the most difficult shot I ever had in my life, and I just messed it up," Els said.

On the other hand, if Els played the eighth again and again the chances are that he would not ace it, so perhaps there was a sense of justice in the way he saved two strokes on one hole only to give them back on another.

—**John Hopkins**

Practice with daughter Samantha

Saving par here on the 11th, Retief Goosen "scrambled well on the second nine" for his 69.

an 85 at Royal St George's and, naturally, missed the 36-hole cut. After his 66, there was little likelihood he would miss again, especially because of his confident manner. Playing alongside Mickelson, among those expected to challenge for the Championship, it was Casey who looked like the more polished player. His chipping and putting outshone the more prominent Mickelson.

Casey opened with a drive that sliced the first fairway, then pitched inside 10 feet and holed the putt. One under. Two routine pars, then he birdied the fourth, not uncommon this day, and pitched to six feet on the eighth. He made the putt, but then lost a stroke at the ninth. Out in 34, two under par, he faced the intimidating homeward nine, playing into the wind.

He began by missing the 10th green but brushed that loose shot aside and chipped into the hole for a birdie 3. Next came the terrifying 11th, with its blind drive into a fairway bordered by prickly, ball-eating gorse. Two well-played shots put him on the green, 30 feet from the hole, and Casey calmly ran it in. He was two under par on a pair of holes that, combined, surrendered only 23 birdies all day. Mickelson played them in one over par, Casey in two under.

Casey lost his second stroke on the 12th, but ran in a 30-foot putt on the 16th for his third birdie of the nine. It had been a struggle. He drove into rough so punishing he played a pitching wedge back to the fairway, then a six iron to the green. Luckily, he holed the putt.

His birdie at the 18th came more easily—a two iron from the tee, eight iron to 16 feet, and another putt dropped. Back in 32, he had his 66 and waited for the field to catch him.

Casey had come into the Championship full of promise, and indeed had built an impressive record

1

Round of the Day

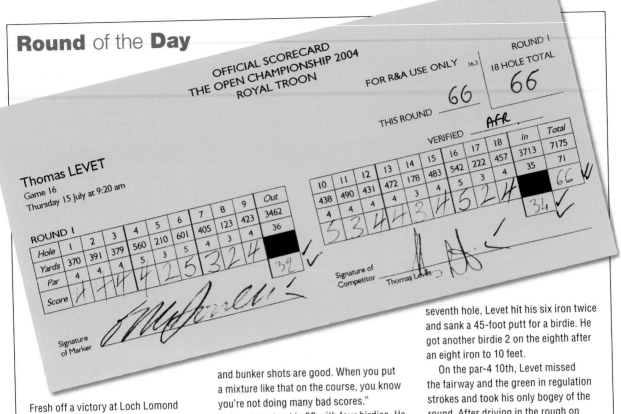

OFFICIAL SCORECARD
THE OPEN CHAMPIONSHIP 2004
ROYAL TROON

FOR R&A USE ONLY 16.3

ROUND 1
18 HOLE TOTAL
66

THIS ROUND — 66

VERIFIED — AFR

Thomas LEVET
Game 16
Thursday 15 July at 9:20 am

	10	11	12	13	14	15	16	17	18	In	Total
	438	490	431	472	178	483	542	222	457	3713	7175
	4	4	4	4	3	4	5	3	4	35	71
	5	3	4	4	3	4	5	2	4	34	66

Signature of Competitor Thomas Levet

ROUND 1

Hole	1	2	3	4	5	6	7	8	9	Out
Yards	370	391	379	560	210	601	405	123	423	3462
Par	4	4	4	5	3	5	4	3	4	36
Score	4	4	4	4	2	5	3	2	4	32

Signature of Marker

Fresh off a victory at Loch Lomond and a day at home in London before travelling back to Scotland, Thomas Levet was rested and confident as The Open got underway. "I know I can shoot low," Levet said after returning a 66, five under par. "My putting, chipping, and bunker shots are good. When you put a mixture like that on the course, you know you're not doing many bad scores."

Levet went out in 32 with four birdies. He reached the green of the par-5 fourth hole with a three wood after using a driver off the tee, and two-putted for his 4. At the fifth, he hit a three-iron shot to 10 feet and holed the putt for birdie 2. At the 405-yard, par-4 seventh hole, Levet hit his six iron twice and sank a 45-foot putt for a birdie. He got another birdie 2 on the eighth after an eight iron to 10 feet.

On the par-4 10th, Levet missed the fairway and the green in regulation strokes and took his only bogey of the round. After driving in the rough on the 11th, he hit a six iron from about 200 yards to 10 feet and holed the putt for birdie 3. His final birdie was on the par-3 17th with a lengthy putt, which he figured to be 33 feet.

My *Favourite* Open

1967 Hoylake

Goran Zachrisson
Swedish television commentator

"Roberto de Vicenzo's Open at Hoylake in 1967 was the loveliest of all. He came from a poor background in Argentina and paved the way for the Romeros and the Cabreras. They never forgot that the game has given them everything."

as an amateur before joining the professional tour. Twice he had won the English Amateur championship, represented Great Britain and Ireland in the 1999 Walker Cup Match, and, although an Englishman, played in the United States for the Arizona State University's golf team, the same university attended by Mickelson, whom he beat this day by seven strokes. He had also erased a number of Mickelson's college records.

He had also been somewhat controversial. Speaking of some other European golfers who haven't had much success, he said, "Too many are content to be journeymen. I want to be on the world stage, playing against the best."

For one round, at least, Casey had left the game's best behind. But he hadn't left Levet behind.

Tiger Woods had consecutive bogeys after missing the fairway off the 13th tee.

Almost A Round From His Dreams

"There were a lot of guys who dreamt of shooting 66 at The Open Championship"

When Colin Montgomerie was at his considerable best, he would often talk of how he felt one up on the first tee. That was how it was for Paul Casey on the morning of the first round. He was staying along the road from Royal Troon and had walked to the course at 7.00 am to meet his coach, Peter Kostis. "Far from worrying about how much time I would need to allow for the traffic, I had this relaxing stroll," Casey said. "It was a very peaceful start to a tournament day."

By the time he had unleashed a series of low and boring shots into an imaginary wind, the one which some had forecast for later in the day, Casey was feeling even better about himself. The practice session over, he and Kostis went their separate ways. Casey was off to the first tee, while Kostis was heading for his flight back to the United States.

Kostis's parting shot—"Have fun out there!"—was not meant in the usual clichéd manner. It was entirely serious, for it was in following that instruction that Casey had ended up with his tie for sixth place at the 2004 Masters Tournament.

Casey's playing companions for the first two rounds at Royal Troon were Shigeki Maruyama and Phil Mickelson. With his omnipresent grin, Maruyama served as a constant reminder to Casey that he should enjoy himself. As for Mickelson, Casey was entirely comfortable in his company. He had attended Mickelson's old university, Arizona State, and had come to know him well. Mickelson had helped him in the art of wedge play, and also had answered his every question about golf and life on the USPGA Tour.

Where Maruyama opened with a 71, and Mickelson 73, Casey came in with a 66 to share the lead with Thomas Levet. This led Casey, prompted by a question from a journalist, to reflect on his good fortune as a successful 26-year-old with three PGA

Of his 67, Paul Casey said, "It could have been very, very low."

European Tour victories since starting as a professional in 2001.

"There were a lot of guys who dreamt of shooting 66 at The Open Championship. Luckily, I'm the one who's doing it," said Casey, who had missed the 36-hole cut in his two previous Opens. "Every 12-year-old dreams of holing putts at The Open and teeing off with Phil Mickelson and Shigeki Maruyama in the first round. I'm very happy with the way things have gone, and the hard work is paying off, because I spent a lot of time hitting golf balls when I was 12 years old and dreaming of this."

Out in 34, Casey had expected to come face-to-face with the wind on the return journey. But the wind never came, and the

player, counting his blessings along with the birdies, was home in the silkiest of 32s. A sand wedge to six feet at the 123-yard eighth had paved the way for his favourite birdie of the day, but the main impression over the 18 holes was one of long driving allied to a wealth of patience.

As is always the way, Casey felt that he had "left quite a few shots out there," with particular reference to a three-footer which got away at the fifth. That apart, his only regret was that Kostis had not been there to see a round which was 19 shots better than his Thursday effort at Royal St George's in 2003.

—Lewine Mair

Air mail from Prestwick passes over the Postage Stamp.

Casey had teed off at 8.30 and Levet 50 minutes later. The French-man had earned his place in The Open field by winning the Barclays Scottish Open the previous week by playing Loch Lomond in 269 strokes and beating par by 15 strokes. He is better known, though, for nearly winning at Muirfield in 2002. He tied Els, Stuart Appleby, and Steve Elkington over the regulation 72 holes, then lost to Els by one stroke in the playoff, on the fifth hole, following the regulation four-hole playoff where Appleby and Elkington were eliminated.

Unlike Casey, Levet made his birdies on the first nine, reaching the fourth green with a well-played three wood and getting down in two putts, then lashing a two iron to 10 feet and birdieing the 210-yard fifth. He made a par 5 at the sixth, then two six irons to the seventh and a 45-foot putt from just off the green for another birdie.

At the eighth, where Els had played a pitching wedge, Levet struck an eight iron to 10 feet and holed still another putt, his fourth birdie in five holes. Out in 32, he lost a stroke at the 10th where his eight iron missed the green, then won it back on the 11th by ripping a 200-yard six iron from the left rough to 10 feet. The putt fell, and Levet went back to four under par.

Levet birdied one more hole, playing a four iron to 33 feet on the 17th, at 222 yards the longest of the par-3s, and holing still another putt. Back in 34, he had matched Casey.

While every group carried substantial galleries, none matched the *esprit de corps* of Montgomerie's. He had teed off just before 9 o'clock, and when he finished, it seemed as if everyone in his gallery had

"Thomas Levet seems like the kind of fellow you would want in your Sunday fourball. He can play, of course he can, but he smiles a lot too, which is a characteristic not often seen in these dour days."

—**Mike Selvey,** *The Guardian*

"The first stage of the catharsis had come at the Association of Golf Writers dinner on Tuesday evening, when Colin Montgomerie looked his critics in the eye and proceeded to charm the socks off them."

—**Neil Harman,** *The Times*

"Tiger Woods left the first round of The Open with a memento and some hope, not necessarily in that order. Along with the golf ball Greg Norman flipped to him on the 18th green—one grinder to another—Woods was encouraged with his best first round in a major in seven tries."

—**Mark Herrmann,** *New York Newsday*

"If the ebbs and flows of his life have centred on lesser tournaments, the high and low tides of Gary Evans's career continue to be set at The Open."

—**Jock MacVicar,** *Daily Express*

"Ben Curtis refused to blame the pressure of returning as defending champion for his four-over-par 75. The American farmer's son, who won as a 500-1 rookie at Sandwich last year, is now struggling to make the cut."

—**Dave Kidd,** *The Sun*

Round One Hole Summary

HOLE	PAR	YARDS	EAGLES	BIRDIES	PARS	BOGEYS	D.BOGEYS	HIGHER	RANK	AVERAGE
1	4	370	1	27	100	21	5	2	13	4.06
2	4	391	0	30	114	10	2	0	16	3.90
3	4	379	0	18	112	20	5	1	11	4.10
4	5	560	4	49	92	9	1	1	17	4.72
5	3	210	0	15	95	44	2	0	8	3.21
6	5	601	4	36	90	21	2	3	15	4.96
7	4	405	0	26	101	23	5	1	12	4.07
8	3	123	1	34	94	23	2	2	14	2.99
9	4	423	0	9	106	37	3	1	4	4.24
OUT	**36**	**3462**	**10**	**244**	**904**	**208**	**27**	**11**		**36.24**
10	4	438	0	12	94	40	10	0	2	4.31
11	4	490	0	11	90	33	16	6	1	4.46
12	4	431	0	9	108	32	7	0	4	4.24
13	4	472	0	10	115	30	1	0	9	4.14
14	3	178	0	12	115	26	3	0	10	3.13
15	4	483	0	11	105	33	7	0	6	4.23
16	5	542	0	67	71	17	1	0	18	4.69
17	3	222	0	16	98	36	5	1	7	3.22
18	4	457	0	18	91	37	9	1	3	4.26
IN	**35**	**3713**	**0**	**166**	**887**	**284**	**59**	**8**		**36.67**
TOTAL	**71**	**7175**	**10**	**410**	**1791**	**492**	**86**	**19**		**72.91**

seen all they wanted to see, and this vast horde marched down a road bordering Royal Troon's late holes against the flow of other spectators heading for refreshment stands and other facilities.

Montgomerie had indeed given them hope. With the cries of "Go, Monty" urging him on, he played rock steady golf through the first nine with only two incidents. Royal Troon's early holes border the beach of the Firth of Clyde where a group of pensioners paraded carrying banners supporting pensioners' rights. As Montgomerie stepped onto the second tee, one of the protesters' mobile phones rang out, a sound that might have turned Monty purple in past times but had no noticeable effect. He simply got on with his game.

Later, about to putt on the eighth, he heard the click of a camera and stepped away, and again got on with the game.

By then Montgomerie had gone three under par by holing from 20 feet on both the second and the fifth, the par-3, pitched to four feet on the sixth and birdied once more.

He had played controlled golf throughout the first nine, but as he made the turn and headed down the 10th, 11th, and 12th, he looked as if his game had collapsed. A wild drive on the 10th followed by an eight iron down a bank over the green led to a 6, and another loose drive at the 11th set up another possibility of a two-stroke loss, but here Monty holed from eight feet and walked off with a bogey 5. Three strokes lost in two holes, and now Montgomerie had gone back to level par for the round.

Naturally he had felt pretty low, but as he approached the 12th tee, the gallery cheered so loudly, fans on other parts of the course assumed

Returning a 73, Phil Mickelson didn't have a birdie until the 16th, and posted three bogeys.

someone had played a spectacular shot. The cheering may have puzzled them, but it boosted Monty.

"That rescued my round," Montgomerie claimed later. "I think it enabled me to go on and break 70, so all credit to them."

Whatever the reason, he immediately picked up one lost stroke with a stunning six iron to four feet that set up a birdie on the 12th and another after a six iron to 20 feet on the 15th. He had recovered two of the three lost strokes and finished his round with 69, just three strokes off the lead.

Then there was Chris DiMarco, a 35-year-old American who lives in Orlando, Florida. He left Orlando Monday afternoon to catch a flight from Philadelphia to Glasgow scheduled to leave at 8.30 pm. Waiting for the Glasgow flight, he and the other passengers found they couldn't board because someone had stuffed a blanket down a toilet, and the airline could not take off unless all the facilities were operational.

They boarded the plane at 3.30 am Tuesday, but by then the flight crew had exceeded their time limit of duty hours and had to be replaced. The passengers then were shunted to various hotels nearby and didn't leave until Tuesday evening.

Instead of flying directly to Glasgow, the airline rerouted DiMarco to Heathrow Airport outside London, then to Glasgow. He arrived at Troon 6.30 Wednesday evening with no luggage and no sleep.

He had his golf bag, though, and the next day bought a shirt, put on the pants to his rainsuit, and teed off at 7.47 Thursday morning.

DiMarco posted a 71, not the lowest round of the day, but it deserved to be ranked among the best.

Second Round

Skipping Over The Stars

By Robert Sommers

The top seven of the world's highest-ranked golfers were filling out the scoreboard but the name at the top was less familiar, Skip Kendall, ranked No 90, who had never won a tournament or even contended in a major championship.

With an impressive field of the leading international golfers such as Ernie Els, Vijay Singh, Retief Goosen, Phil Mickelson, Mike Weir, Kenny Perry, Davis Love III, and—lest we forget—Tiger Woods closing in on the leaders, the second round of The Open Championship was completed with the American journeyman Skip Kendall taking over first place from Paul Casey and Thomas Levet.

Kendall played Royal Troon in 66 strokes and moved to the top of the scoreboard with a 36-hole total of 135, seven under the par of 71. Playing about an hour behind Kendall in the afternoon, Levet added a 70 to his opening 66, and at 136 fell

---

Colin Montgomerie delighted his supporters with a second 69.

into second place. Casey, the other leader of the first round, took a 77 and dropped all the way to a tie for 37th place at 143.

Barry Lane added 68 to his opening 69 and shared third place with K J Choi, at 137. Choi had scores of 68 and then 69.

While his Scottish supporters rocked the heavens cheering him on, Colin Montgomerie went round in another 69 and, at 138, tied for fifth place with Els, Singh, Michael Campbell, and another American, Todd Hamilton, whose 67 stood as the second lowest score of the day.

Others made their moves as well. Shrugging off his disappointing 73 of the previous day, Mickelson birdied four of the first six holes, matched Kendall's 66, and climbed into a tie for 10th place at 139 in a group with Goosen, Weir, Perry, and Scott Verplank. Even though with 71 Woods scored one stroke higher than his opening round, he climbed from a tie for 26th into a tie for 17th at 141. Obviously old Troon still had sharp teeth.

Trouser legs flapped in the freshening breeze and the flags flying atop the big grandstands snapped in the smart breeze as golfers struggled playing shots

Barry Lane finished in 68 with birdie putts of 20 and 25 feet on the last two holes.

through the crosswinds. While this was not wind at its wildest, as we are likely to see at Royal Troon, it whipped in strong enough to cause grief.

Weir, the left-handed Canadian who had won the Masters Tournament a year earlier, claimed he played a significant number of drawn shots going out because the wind came off the Clyde, blowing right to left, then coming back he had to fade the ball, once again fighting the left-to-right wind. Of course, for most of the field, it was just the opposite.

Others, such as Casey, found the breeze too much to handle. Carl Pettersson, who had opened with 68, matched Casey's 77. Matthew Goggin dropped further, from 68 to 78 and missed the 36-hole cut.

The cut fell at 145, three over par. Some great players of the past,

Second Round Leaders

HOLE	1	2	3	4	5	6	7	8	9	10	11	12	13	14	15	16	17	18	TOTAL
PAR	4	4	4	5	3	5	4	3	4	4	4	4	4	3	4	5	3	4	TOTAL
Skip Kendall	4	4	(3)	5	(2)	5	4	3	4	4	[5]	(3)	4	(2)	4	(3)	3	4	66-135
Thomas Levet	4	(3)	4	(4)	3	5	4	3	4	4	4	[5]	4	3	4	5	3	4	70-136
Barry Lane	4	(3)	[5]	[6]	(2)	[6]	4	(2)	4	4	4	(3)	4	3	4	5	(2)	(3)	68-137
K J Choi	4	(3)	4	5	3	5	(3)	[4]	4	4	[5]	(3)	4	3	4	(4)	3	4	69-137
Michael Campbell	(3)	[5]	4	5	3	5	4	(2)	4	[5]	4	[5]	(3)	3	4	5	3	4	71-138
Vijay Singh	4	(3)	4	5	[4]	5	(3)	3	[5]	4	4	4	4	3	4	(4)	3	4	70-138
Todd Hamilton	(3)	[5]	4	5	3	(4)	(2)	3	4	[5]	4	(3)	4	3	4	(4)	3	4	67-138
Ernie Els	4	4	4	5	[4]	(4)	4	3	4	(3)	4	4	[5]	(2)	4	(4)	3	4	69-138
Colin Montgomerie	(3)	(3)	[5]	(4)	3	5	4	3	[5]	4	4	4	4	3	(3)	(4)	3	[5]	69-138
Mike Weir	4	4	4	5	(2)	(4)	(3)	3	[5]	4	4	4	4	3	4	(4)	3	4	68-139
Kenny Perry	4	4	[5]	(4)	(2)	[6]	4	[5]	4	[5]	4	4	4	(2)	(3)	(4)	3	(3)	70-139
Retief Goosen	4	4	4	5	3	5	(3)	3	4	4	4	4	4	3	4	5	3	4	70-139
Phil Mickelson	(3)	4	(3)	(4)	3	(4)	4	3	4	4	4	4	4	3	4	(4)	3	4	66-139
Scott Verplank	4	(3)	4	5	3	(4)	4	3	4	4	4	4	4	3	4	5	[4]	4	70-139

Official World Golf Ranking

As of 12 July 2004

Players in **bold** within the leading 20 players (and ties) after 36 holes

	Player	Points
1.	**Tiger Woods**	12.05
2.	**Ernie Els**	10.73
3.	**Vijay Singh**	10.30
4.	**Phil Mickelson**	7.97
5.	**Davis Love III**	7.68
6.	**Retief Goosen**	7.30
7.	**Mike Weir**	6.49
8.	Padraig Harrington	5.82
9.	Jim Furyk	5.51
10.	Sergio Garcia	5.04
11.	**Adam Scott**	4.84
12.	**Kenny Perry**	4.84
13.	Chad Campbell	4.83
14.	Stuart Appleby	4.51
15.	**Darren Clarke**	4.35

K J Choi said Royal Troon "fits me very well" and was similar to his home course by the ocean in Korea.

An eagle at the 16th put Skip Kendall in first place.

among them seven former champions, would not finish the 72 holes. The victims included Ben Curtis, the surprise Open champion of 2003. Curtis showed little of the command of his shots he had under the milder weather at Sandwich, followed his opening 75 with 74, and at 149 missed by four strokes.

On the other hand, Chris DiMarco, after a good night's sleep, arrived at Royal Troon appropriately dressed; his luggage had arrived Thursday evening from who knows where. He went round in another 71, and at 142 survived the cut with ease.

Campbell had come within a stroke of tying John Daly and Costantino Rocca for first place in the 1995 Open at St Andrews, and now he played Royal Troon in 71 strokes, which, added to his opening 67, moved him into the lead early in the day at 138. It didn't last, of course.

Until his surprising 66, Kendall had given no indication he would play so well under the tension of the game's greatest moment, yet he had done reasonably well a month earlier by tying for 17th place in the US Open.

Still, Kendall had played the USPGA Tour for 10 years and gone through 310 tournaments without winning anything but lots of money. He had come close early in the season, but lost a playoff to Mickelson in the Bob Hope Chrysler Classic. He had also tied for fifth at the Bank of America Colonial later in the year, but he had missed eight cuts in 18 starts.

This was only the 14th major championship of Kendall's career, and his third Open. He missed the cut in 1998 and tied for 59th last year. His best finish ever in a major event was a tie for 10th in the 1998 USPGA Championship.

None of this seemed to matter when Kendall birdied two of Royal Troon's first five holes, his first on the third hole where his wedge approach kicked left into a greenside bunker and he holed his recovery, and his second on the fifth with a stunning four iron that couldn't have stopped farther

SKIP KENDALL

He Turns The Tables

Early in his professional career, he even worked as a waiter in a restaurant in Florida

Anyone passing the first tee in the moments before his starting time of 1.20 pm on Friday might not have given Skip Kendall a second glance. Unless spectators knew to the contrary, they might have thought that he was too small and too slight to tangle with a monster of a course such as Royal Troon on a windy day. Kendall is 5ft 8in, weighed 10½ stone at The Open, and has something of the schoolboy about his face. He looks as though a gust of wind would blow him over.

On the eve of The Open, Tiger Woods had said that the winner would be the one who controlled his golf ball best, and in the second round it was Kendall, a man without a victory on the USPGA Tour, who did this best.

Kendall's 66, seven strokes better than the average score of the day of 73.55, was the lowest of the day, one equalled by Phil Mickelson, and gave him the outright lead after 36 holes by one stroke.

Kendall said he thought it was going to be his day when he holed from a bunker on the third for the first of his four birdies, and knew it was going to be his day when he holed a 50-foot putt for an eagle 3 on the 16th.

He is more than a good golfer. He is interesting, generous, and loyal to his mother. Not many professionals run a charity pro-am and support a children's hospital. Few had brought their 80-year-old mother over to Scotland with them as he had. And no one had taken a large cut into their left index finger as Kendall had done when slicing a frozen breakfast bagel in May the previous year, had it sewn back on, and, by adopting a different grip, was soon able to play competitive golf again.

As if this were not enough to mark Kendall out, he explained how during the first round of The Open he had run the risk of being exiled to the Tower of London by wandering over to His Royal Highness the Duke of York, who is the current captain of

The Royal and Ancient Golf Club of St Andrews, sticking his hand out and saying, "Hi, I'm Skip Kendall."

Kendall got the last qualifying place at Congressional when the last of the International Final Qualifying competitions was held there. He said that he had been helped at Troon by playing in the US Open at Shinnecock Hills where he had tied for 17th a few weeks earlier. "I'm getting used to using my imagination a little more and learning what you can do and can't do on certain shots," Kendall said.

He recalled how early in his professional career he had worked as a waiter in a restaurant in Orlando to eke out a living while playing on the mini tours around Florida. "Some days I had to work the lunch and dinner shift," Kendall said. "So in between shifts I would go to a field that was near the restaurant and hit balls. I kept my bow tie on because it was too hard to take off and put back on again."

The moral of this story is clear: Anyone who is prepared to practise in a field while wearing a bow tie is not going to be put off their game by a wind, and on this day, if not later, Kendall was not.

—**John Hopkins**

It was a beautiful day for golf in Ayrshire.

A French Accent On Troon

A linguist capable of conversing in many tongues as well as a golfer who can play just about anywhere, the fact France's Thomas Levet, winner of the Barclays Scottish Open, can speak German, English, Spanish, and a little bit of Swedish and Japanese, impressed the locals much less than his grasp of the vernacular. Asked if he knew any Scottish phrases, Levet replied, "Yes, I know in Aberdeen they say 'Fit like, man?', which means 'How are you doing?'"

Not since the Granite City's Paul Lawrie won The Open at Carnoustie had a potential Open champion emerged who knew the meaning of "Fit like". Levet's second round of 70 for a six-under-par total of 136 for second place at the halfway mark of the Championship had already cemented the Frenchman's reputation in Scottish eyes as a fine competitor. His knowledge of the Doric duly turned admiration into affection for an adopted son.

Ever since Jean Van de Velde came to grief at the 1999 Open, the profile of French golfers at The Open has not been higher since Arnaud Massy won at Hoylake in 1907. Levet himself, of course, was among the runners-up at Muirfield in 2002 after a playoff won by Ernie Els. "I proved to myself at Muirfield that I can do it, that I can compete at this level," said Levet, who has three career victories in Europe.

The Frenchman's liking for Scotland was evident again during 2004. Not only did he win at Loch Lomond the previous week, his name rarely strayed from the leaderboard at Royal Troon. On Friday, the 35-year-old Parisian, who lives in England, made a couple of birdies over the first nine and dropped just one shot to par on the way back when he missed the 12th green.

Three of Levet's countrymen were triumphant on the 2004 PGA European Tour prior to The Open: Jean-Francois Remesy in the French Open, Philippe Lima in the Aa St Omer Open, and Christian Cevaer in the Canarias Open de Espana. Levet, Remesy, Cevaer, and Raphael Jacquelin all competed in Ayrshire and only Remesy missed the cut. Even Van de Velde was on hand working as a television commentator for the BBC.

Thomas Levet said he wanted to play a good round and not think about the lead.

Working with Jos Vanstiphout, the same Belgian sports psychologist who did so much for Els and Retief Goosen, Levet was able to call on a remarkably high level of confidence at Loch Lomond when he bolted through the field on the final day thanks to a remarkable performance with the putter.

Apart from taking home a cheque for £366,660, Levet earned a spot in The Open as the highest non-exempt finisher. After nipping home to potter in his garden for a day and watch his children play tennis, the Frenchman returned to Scotland feeling good about things. "You get a lot of rewards from this game," he said. "It's a nice life."

Levet was not always so even-keeled and drew a comparison with the volatile tennis player, Goran Ivanisevic. "I can be good Thomas and bad Thomas," he admitted, before recalling Trevor Immelman's story about playing with a golfer who hit a wedge to 10 feet and missed the next four putts. The golfer was so incensed he knocked the ball back off the green, hit another chip to 10 feet and holed the putt for 10. "That was me," Levet confessed.

—**Mike Aitken**

Vijay Singh was happy with 70 to be four under par.

Ernie Els said, "69 is never a bad score."

than two feet from the hole for the 2.

Yet it was on the second nine where Kendall played his best, even though he lost a stroke on the merciless 11th because of a wayward drive in the gorse. Clearly the ball was unplayable, so Kendall took a penalty stroke and dropped clear.

His was a hard-won bogey 5 there. His nearest point of relief kept his ball behind the gorse bushes, forcing him to play over them. His four iron missed the green to the left, and he chipped to five feet and made the putt.

"That helped," he conceded.

As if retaliating for an insult, Kendall struck back by playing a seven-iron approach into the 12th, which is not the easiest of holes, and running in a 25-foot putt for one birdie, a six iron into the 178-yard 14th and holing from 15 feet for another, then capped his round on the 16th, the last of the par-5s, playing a two iron from the tee and a three wood from the fairway that stopped barely short of the putting surface. Reading the break perfectly, Kendall holed from 50 feet.

As a physical specimen, Kendall falls short of imposing. A slightly

> **My** *Favourite*
> ## Open
>
> ### 2002 Muirfield
>
> **David Pepper**
> Chairman of Championship
> Committee
>
> "Ernie Els seemed clearly distressed when he finished the 72nd hole after losing two strokes on the 16th. Waiting to tee off in the playoff, he stood for about 10 minutes composing himself by eating a sandwich whilst the group ahead played out of range. I've often wondered what would have happened if he had been drawn to play first."

Round of the **Day**

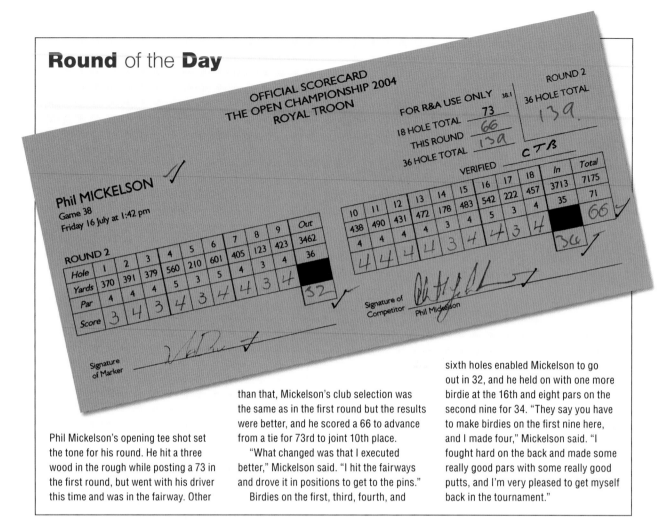

OFFICIAL SCORECARD
THE OPEN CHAMPIONSHIP 2004
ROYAL TROON

FOR R&A USE ONLY   38.1

	ROUND 2
18 HOLE TOTAL	73
THIS ROUND	66
36 HOLE TOTAL	139
36 HOLE TOTAL	139

VERIFIED   CTB

Phil MICKELSON ✓
Game 38
Friday 16 July at 1:42 pm

ROUND 2

Hole	1	2	3	4	5	6	7	8	9	Out
Yards	370	391	379	560	210	601	405	123	423	3462
Par	4	4	4	5	3	5	4	3	4	36
Score	3	4	3	4	3	4	4	3	4	32

Hole	10	11	12	13	14	15	16	17	18	In	Total
Yards	438	490	431	472	178	483	542	222	457	3713	7175
Par	4	4	4	4	3	4	5	3	4	35	71
Score	4	4	4	4	3	4	4	3	4	34	66

Signature of Competitor   *Phil Mickelson*

Signature of Marker

Phil Mickelson's opening tee shot set the tone for his round. He hit a three wood in the rough while posting a 73 in the first round, but went with his driver this time and was in the fairway. Other than that, Mickelson's club selection was the same as in the first round but the results were better, and he scored a 66 to advance from a tie for 73rd to joint 10th place.

"What changed was that I executed better," Mickelson said. "I hit the fairways and drove it in positions to get to the pins."

Birdies on the first, third, fourth, and sixth holes enabled Mickelson to go out in 32, and he held on with one more birdie at the 16th and eight pars on the second nine for 34. "They say you have to make birdies on the first nine here, and I made four," Mickelson said. "I fought hard on the back and made some really good pars with some really good putts, and I'm very pleased to get myself back in the tournament."

At 139, Scott Verplank was off to his best start in eight Opens.

built man of about 10½ stone and standing 5ft 8in, at age 39 he is beginning to lose his hair. Remarkably, a year earlier he had nearly lost a sizeable part of his left index finger as well. While he was playing in the Memorial Tournament, in Dublin, Ohio, he had tried to slice into a frozen bagel, but as he began cutting, the bagel slipped on the cutting board. The knife—quite a sharp knife—sliced off a piece of his finger.

"I didn't cut it completely off," Kendall explained, "but I cut a big piece of it off, and they (doctors at a hospital) had to sew it back on.

"I didn't play for about four weeks, but I came back playing probably better with a new grip. So maybe it was a blessing. But I'm back now, all 10 digits are back intact."

While Kendall knew he led the field, he knew as well that Levet had closed to within a stroke of him with his round of 70. And Levet had played a few holes under the burden of not knowing if he would be penalised for a rules infraction he hadn't prevented.

Pulling his opening drive badly—the ball settled near an ice cream truck behind steel fencing—Levet saw a few marshals remove sections of the fence from his line of play while a referee, possibly distracted by another player's even wilder drive, stood by. Of course, allowing your line of play to be improved violates the Rules of Golf, which meant that Levet may had been penalised two strokes.

Made aware of the circumstances, officials conferred with one another, and after Levet had played to the fifth hole, he learned that he had been excused. None of this apparently distracted Levet from the job in hand. Instead, he played first-class golf throughout the first nine, and with a little better luck might have birdied more than the two holes he managed.

While the issue of a possible penalty must have bothered him, he hit every fairway except the first, and every green going out. Yet his steady ball-striking won him very little. He birdied only the second, playing a seven iron into the green and holing from 30 feet, and the par-5 fourth, reaching a greenside bunker and pitching to 10 feet.

The more difficult inward nine cost him one stroke. Once more the 12th caused the damage. He hit the fairway nicely, pulled his nine-iron approach left of the green, and his chip wasn't nearly good enough. He took two more to hole out.

Speaking of the possible penalty later, Levet gave the impression he didn't feel concerned.

"At this time," he said, "I was, I think, two in front, so I would be tied for the lead. When you're in the position of leading the tournament, it doesn't matter," which seems a strange comment. But then Levet isn't your conventional golfer.

Todd Hamilton, on the way to a 67, acknowledged the applause at the 17th for his par.

Low Scores	
Low First Nine	
Phil Mickelson	32
Stewart Cink	32
Low Second Nine	
Brad Faxon	31
Paul Bradshaw	31
Low Round	
Skip Kendall	66
Phil Mickelson	66

After dropping shots on the 10th and 12th, Michael Campbell struck an eight iron to 25 feet here at the 13th for a birdie.

"A golf shot is only a golf shot," Levet has said. "It can't change your life."

One behind Levet on the scoreboard, Lane was also not following the usual route. He had revived his game at the age of 44, winning earlier this year in the Daily Telegraph Damovo British Masters, his first victory in 10 years. "The older you get, the harder it gets," Lane said. "Now I'm working harder, and it's paying dividends."

For his 68, Lane was level par on the first nine, with three birdies offset by three bogeys. He played the inward nine in 32, making a birdie from 10 feet on the 12th and then holing putts of 20 and 25 feet for birdies on the last two holes.

Choi also putted well for his 69 to tie Lane at 137, his final two birdies coming from 30 feet on the 12th and 15 feet on the 16th hole.

Montgomerie had to qualify for The Open at Sunningdale. It would have been a shame had he missed, because he considered Troon to be his hometown, and for many years his father had been secretary of the club. Monty had learned to play on this very course, and as he reminded the rest of the field, "I know it better than anyone else, and they know that I know they know." As a native son, Montgomerie drew devoted and passionate galleries. When he walked onto the first tee for his 2.09 starting time, spectators packing the grandstand rose and seemed to stand at attention, as if honouring a national hero.

Montgomerie rewarded them with a stirring beginning. He holed from 25 feet and birdied the first, then laid his approach inside 10 feet and birdied the second as well.

His upward movement stalled when he lost a stroke at the third, but he fought back, caught a

Colin Montgomerie took a bogey here at the 18th.

Excerpts FROM THE Press

"Short of carrying him down the fairways like an ancient Scottish king, it's hard to see what more the West Coast clan can do to help Colin Montgomerie win this Open Championship."

—**Paul Hayward**, *The Daily Telegraph*

"Winning a major championship is never easy. But as Skip Kendall takes a surprising one-stroke lead into the third round of The Open, the ghosts of Kendall's past, and the talent of the players chasing him, may ruin the opportunity of a lifetime."

—**Clifton Brown**, *The New York Times*

"On a day of strong crosswinds, a consistent round by Retief Goosen lifted him up the leaderboard and within sight of adding The Open to the US Open crown he landed last month."

—**Douglas Lowe**, *The Herald*

"As the wind finally stirred and started to give people trouble, seven former Open champions led the long parade of those who missed the cut, with Paul Lawrie, the last Briton to win the title, having the most torrid time of the lot."

—**Mel Webb**, *The Times*

"In an event that drips with tradition, where legends are born and champions are worshipped, Phil Mickelson and Colin Montgomerie are trying to dispel a couple of myths."

—**John Davis**, *Arizona Republic*

Phil Mickelson equalled the day's low score with 66, including five birdies.

greenside bunker at the fourth but recovered close enough to hole a putt, and once again went back to two under par for the round.

By now the gallery had almost reached the point of frenzy, crying, "Go, Monty," raising fists skyward, waving the cross of St Andrew, Scotland's national flag, and rushing ahead to catch a glimpse of every shot. But once again Montgomerie lost momentum.

He bogeyed the ninth, and a 12-foot putt for a birdie on the 14th seemed ready to drop but instead hung on the edge. He missed the fairway of the 15th, yet drilled his approach within 15 feet and holed for a birdie. On to the 16th.

Playing a safe iron off the tee, even though this was a par-5, Montgomerie tore into a three-wood second and ran the ball off the back of the green. He nearly holed his chip. The ball grazed the edge but wouldn't fall. Still, another birdie, and now Monty stood three under par with just two holes to play.

Mickelson
A New Attention To Detail

By Andy Farrell

That a new Phil Mickelson had arrived at The Open Championship this year was evident almost as soon as the American touched down on British soil on the day prior to the start of the Barclays Scottish Open. Instead of going to Loch Lomond, where he would be playing the following day, Mickelson went straight to Royal Troon, where he would be playing the following week.

A new attention to detail had brought success in the major championships where previously the outrageously talented left-hander had only been left disappointed on the game's grandest occasions. After 46 majors without a victory, Mickelson won the Masters Tournament at Augusta in April with five birdies in the last seven holes to defeat Ernie Els by one stroke in a thrilling duel.

In June, at the US Open, only Mickelson and Retief Goosen could handle the severity of the Shinnecock Hills course on the final day. Even though the American lost out to the South African in another tense encounter, this time a near-miss only emphasised that Mickelson was on the right track. Suddenly, he was not the man without a major, but the man to beat to win a major.

Yet, although the 34-year-old had collected 19 top-10 finishes in the majors, none had come at The Open. His best result was tied for 11th in 2000 at St Andrews, where he finished 12 strokes behind Tiger Woods.

With so much shot-making ability and imagination at his command, this was always puzzling. But being high, and all too often wide and not very handsome, off the tee had always killed his chances on the links. A 73 on the opening day at Royal Troon suggested his failure to get into contention at The Open would continue. A 66 on Friday was an emphatic rebuttal.

This new Mickelson might have arrived earlier had he not been so stubborn. While the rest of the golfing world thought he needed to tighten up when the examination was at its most severe, the American resolutely maintained he played his best when challenging himself to be aggressive and daring.

The Road to Damascus moment came during 2003, when he did not win a title and lost every match at the Presidents Cup. But his year was overshadowed by the birth of his son Evan. Due to complications both baby and mother spent four days in intensive care. The whole family took time to recover, and such incidents put things like golf in perspective.

Writing off 2003, Mickelson started afresh on New Year's Day. A fitness regime was new, while finally he allowed Rick Smith, his coach, to do whatever remedial work he thought necessary on the swing. Shorter and smoother, Mickelson had an action that allowed him to hit more fairways and more greens, which, he found, could be fun, too.

"I still want to be aggressive," he said, "but from the middle of the fairway rather than the tee." Dave Pelz, a former NASA scientist who is now a short-game expert, worked on the shots Mickelson needed to become more successful from 150 yards and in, rather than just showy.

Before both the Masters and the US Open, Mickelson, Smith, and Pelz spent three days at the venue working on a strategy that could save him half a shot to a shot a round. "That's what you need to go from being in contention to being on top," Mickelson said.

"I prepared very hard for Shinnecock and felt I would have a good chance as the week started. The harder the course, the more my preparation seems to help. I feel very confident in how I am playing."

Mickelson missed the 36-hole cut at Loch Lomond and admitted he was thinking more about what he needed to do to prepare for Troon and the challenge of links golf.

"In the past I did not feel comfortable with the types of shots you need here, meaning less spin, lower flight, letting the ball run up. I feel more comfortable now and I'm expecting to use many of the shots I have worked on throughout the year.

"But I also feel there is an element of luck needed to do well in a major championship, whether it's which side of the draw you are on for the first two days, hitting the flagstick when you might have gone through the green, or having (Chris) DiMarco putting on the same line (on the final green) at Augusta. You can't control the breaks, but you can control the preparation and the style of shots you hit."

Playing in the slightly easier conditions on Friday afternoon, Mickelson was less tentative than the previous day and birdied the first and the third, the fourth and the sixth to take advantage of the chances on offer on the first nine. Coming home he parred in with the exception of a 4 at the par-5 16th to equal his lowest score in The Open, a 66 in the second round at St Andrews in 2000.

He was still four strokes off the lead and acknowledged he had a lot of work still to do. But, ominously, he had not dropped a stroke, and the only other player to manage that in the second round was Goosen.

"What I love about the majors," Mickelson added, "is the variety of golf required. At Augusta, we need power but also finesse around the greens. In a US Open you have to drive the ball well and hit accurate shots to the greens, but the short game is not so important. At The Open you have to control the trajectory, use a variety of shots around the green, and putt well in the wind, which is extremely difficult. If you can win them all, what a complete player you have proven to be."

Retief Goosen welcomed the tougher conditions because "the better players will come to the top."

Collecting autographs must be tiring.

Safely past the dangerous 17th, Montgomerie drove into the rough on the home hole, and his approach rolled dead on the front of the green, leaving him a very long putt. His first died within four feet of the hole, and he missed the second. A bogey 5 on the last, and Montgomerie had his second 69.

The bogey didn't matter to his gallery. Once again his supporters in the stands stood and cheered. Their hometown man still had a chance to win The Open. In the end it would be up to him, but could he do it?

Montgomerie had been a top-10 player in the Official World Golf Ranking for nine years, 1994 through 2002, but by now had slipped below even the top 50 in the world. He won earlier in the year, however, in the Caltex Singapore Masters, an official event on the PGA European Tour.

While so much attention had been lavished on the game's more prominent players, Hamilton turned in a quiet 67 that assured he would be among the last starters in the third round. He stood just two strokes behind Kendall, then confided that he hadn't played well over the last two or three months, and that he feels comfortable even when he doesn't hit a lot of good shots.

Players Below Par	28
Players At Par	17
Players Above Par	111

The winds made for an interesting day of golf—and sailing—along and on the Firth of Clyde.

Gary Evans (far left) played the second, third, and fourth in 15 strokes, five more than in the first round.

Mike Weir (left) built his 68 on consecutive birdies on the fifth, sixth, and seventh holes.

Adam Scott returned a 68, including this save for par from a bunker at the Postage Stamp.

Stewart Cink went out in 32, then gave back all four strokes.

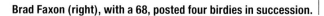

Brad Faxon (right), with a 68, posted four birdies in succession.

Well, he hit enough of them this day, especially his sand wedge pitch to the seventh that ran into the hole for an eagle 2.

Hamilton admitted he hit a poor drive. His ball drifted into the rough about 15 yards right of the fairway and about 120 yards short of the green. His wedge flew out of the grass with no spin, ran to the back of the green and into the hole.

Since he had just birdied the sixth by holing from 12 feet, his eagle on the seventh had dropped him to three under par.

Out in 33, Hamilton missed the 10th green with a nine iron and bogeyed, but reaching the 12th tee, he drove with what he calls his hybrid club. Shaped somewhat like a small-headed wooden club, but, as all modern woods, made of metal, the hybrid can be used for all sorts of purposes. Hamilton drives with it, plays fairway shots with it, and even uses it for work around the greens, such as running shots. He used it at Royal Troon about five times a round.

In its original form his hybrid club had a loft of 17 degrees, roughly the loft of a two iron. By having the hosel bent, Hamilton lowered the loft to 14 degrees, the rough equivalent of the modern three wood in tour players' bags. Whatever its pedigree, it worked for him.

In the rough on the 12th, Hamilton followed with a six iron to 25 feet and holed. Back to three under. Three more pars followed, two of them routine, before he birdied

Darren Clarke (above left) dropped shots on the 16th and 17th.

Tiger Woods (above right) holed a birdie putt on the fourth after reaching the green in three.

2

"Over the past two years Darren Clarke has worked hard on his weight and his patience. It is an ongoing tussle. Through diligent attention to diet he is no longer a fat golfer, but there is still room for improvements in temperament."

—Ken Jones, *The Independent*

"The least known name on the leaderboard belongs to Todd Hamilton. The man from the banks of the Mississippi thrilled the spectators with his golf, and his stories afterwards were equally entertaining."

—Mark Fleming, *Daily Express*

"Brad Faxon's mind started wandering when he made three straight bogeys and soared to six over par through the first 22 holes of The Open. 'I bogeyed 2-3-4 and I was wondering whether there was a Glasgow to Boston non-stop,' said Faxon."

—Joe Gordon, *Boston Herald*

"At times it seems as if everyone in this corner of Ayrshire knows everybody else. Marshals nod to greenkeepers who say hello to caddies who acknowledge friends in the galleries."

—Paul Kelso, *The Guardian*

"Ian Poulter's one-over-par halfway total ensured he will be here for the weekend, and that means more delights from his wardrobe for the watching public."

—Neil Silver, *The Scotsman*

Stuart Appleby posted a 70 despite a bogey at the 18th hole.

one more hole. From the tee of the 542-yard 16th, Hamilton played a two iron, then laid up with a seven iron, and finally a wedge to eight feet. The putt fell, and Hamilton walked away four under par for the 36 holes.

Hamilton's score was one of three rounds of 67. The others were by Australian Kim Felton, who tied for 15th place at 140, and Englishman Paul Bradshaw, who tied for 24th with level-par 142. Bradshaw had 31 on the inward nine, a score matched by Brad Faxon, who posted four birdies in succession starting at the 11th. Faxon returned a 68 and was also at 142. Stewart Cink shot 32 to share the low first nine with Mickelson, but Cink came back in 39 and was at 143.

At the same time, nothing seemed to work as well for Woods as it had a few years earlier. While he manoeuvered himself round Royal Troon in level-par 71, he had not struck fear into anyone's heart for some time. And there was no denying that his presence alone back then intimidated the rest of the field, a psychological advantage worth a few strokes.

Nevertheless, at 141 he found himself within six strokes of Kendall, and, he claimed, liked his position.

"I love it," he said. "With the wind blowing like this, none of the guys are going to run away with it, so I'm right there with a chance going into the weekend."

Still, with Singh, Els, Mickelson, Goosen, Weir, Perry, and Montgomerie between him and first place, he would need more than bravado to pass them all.

Round Two Hole Summary

HOLE	PAR	YARDS	EAGLES	BIRDIES	PARS	BOGEYS	D.BOGEYS	HIGHER	RANK	AVERAGE
1	4	370	0	18	110	23	5	0	14	4.10
2	4	391	0	16	107	26	6	1	9	4.16
3	4	379	1	22	92	34	6	1	9	4.16
4	5	560	0	52	85	15	3	1	17	4.82
5	3	210	0	23	92	40	1	0	11	3.12
6	5	601	0	29	89	36	1	1	15	5.08
7	4	405	1	34	92	27	2	0	16	3.97
8	3	123	0	31	90	24	10	1	13	3.11
9	4	423	0	9	99	39	9	0	3	4.31
OUT	**36**	**3462**	**2**	**234**	**856**	**264**	**43**	**5**		**36.82**
10	4	438	0	13	97	43	1	2	5	4.24
11	4	490	0	16	83	38	15	4	1	4.42
12	4	431	0	16	84	42	11	3	2	4.37
13	4	472	0	8	117	28	3	0	7	4.17
14	3	178	0	9	123	21	3	0	12	3.12
15	4	483	0	13	100	34	5	4	4	4.28
16	5	542	2	54	84	14	1	1	18	4.76
17	3	222	0	11	103	39	3	0	6	3.22
18	4	457	0	16	103	33	3	1	7	4.17
IN	**35**	**3713**	**2**	**156**	**894**	**292**	**45**	**15**		**36.73**
TOTAL	**71**	**7175**	**4**	**390**	**1750**	**556**	**88**	**20**		**72.55**

Paul Bradshaw (far left) had an inward nine of 31 with four birdies.

Davis Love III (left) came in with 69 to tie for 17th place.

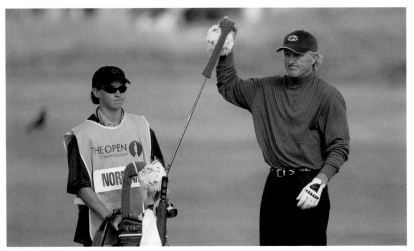

With son Gregory on his bag, Greg Norman (above) missed the cut for the first time since 1980. Tom Weiskopf (below) said he enjoyed returning to the venue of his 1973 victory, despite posting two rounds of 80.

He would not have to pass Curtis, of course, nor Greg Norman, nor Nick Faldo, Paul Lawrie, Tom Lehman, John Daly, nor Tom Weiskopf, who won at Troon in 1973. Now 61 years old, Weiskopf had two rounds of 80.

Thomas Bjorn missed the cut as well, along with Jim Furyk, the 2003 US Open champion, Padraig Harrington, who had played so well on the recent big occasions, and Sergio Garcia.

With two rounds of 73, playing in the final group of the evening, a Swede by the name of Klas Eriksson missed as well, and found a solution. Standing alongside the 18th green, he snapped the shaft of his putter over his knee and proclaimed, "I've been thinking of doing it for three weeks."

Ben Curtis contemplated an early flight home.

Catch Me If You Can

By Robert Sommers

The challenge came from Todd Hamilton, the veteran of Asia and Japan, a first-time winner in America at the age of 38, but leading for the first time in one of the game's great events.

As The Open Championship began three days earlier, hardly anyone could have expected Todd Hamilton to lead the field into the final day, including Hamilton himself.

Yet there he stood in first place after a second consecutive round of 67 over a course that had torn the hearts from so many fine golfers over the years. Hamilton was at 205 for the 54 holes, yet his grip on first place hardly assured he would win, for behind him followed three of the game's more dangerous threats.

Ernie Els, the 2002 champion, lurked one stroke behind, at 206 after his round of 68, and one behind him, at 207, lay Phil Mickelson, winner of the Mas-

---

Phil Mickelson and others seemed ready to pounce.

ters Tournament in April, Retief Goosen, Els's fellow countryman and the reigning US Open champion, and Thomas Levet, who had hung on since the first round. Mickelson and Goosen turned in 68s and Levet added 71 in his series of ascending scores. At 208, Barry Lane held sixth place alone.

At 207, Mickelson, Goosen, and Levet need make up only two strokes on Hamilton, a player untried on the great occasions. Hamilton had won a tournament in America early in the season, but he had not so far reached this stage of an event so important as The Open Championship.

Tiger Woods had won quite a few of them, of course, and when he breezed round Royal Troon in 68 as well, he leaped 10 places, from a tie for 17th into a tie for seventh. More importantly, he raised himself to within four strokes of Hamilton. Had this been two years earlier, it might have been assumed that all was lost, that four strokes hardly stood as a barrier between Woods and the Championship. But no longer did Woods cause those ahead of him to panic.

While Woods moved upward, Colin Montgomerie headed downward with a dull 72, once again

3

Third Round Leaders

HOLE	1	2	3	4	5	6	7	8	9	10	11	12	13	14	15	16	17	18	
PAR	4	4	4	5	3	5	4	3	4	4	4	4	4	3	4	5	3	4	TOTAL
Todd Hamilton	4	4	4	4	3	4	4	2	4	4	4	4	4	2	4	5	3	4	67-205
Ernie Els	3	4	4	5	3	4	4	4	4	4	5	4	3	3	3	4	3	4	68-206
Phil Mickelson	3	3	4	5	3	5	3	3	4	4	4	4	4	3	4	5	3	4	68-207
Retief Goosen	4	4	3	4	4	4	5	3	3	4	3	5	4	3	4	4	3	4	68-207
Thomas Levet	4	4	3	5	2	4	4	3	4	4	6	4	4	3	4	6	3	4	71-207
Barry Lane	4	5	4	5	3	4	4	2	4	5	4	3	3	3	3	5	5	5	71-208
Tiger Woods	3	3	4	4	3	5	3	3	4	4	4	5	4	3	4	5	3	4	68-209
Scott Verplank	4	3	4	4	3	6	3	3	4	5	5	5	4	2	4	4	3	4	70-209
Mike Weir	5	4	4	4	3	5	3	3	4	5	5	4	4	3	5	4	3	3	71-210
Colin Montgomerie	4	4	5	4	4	5	3	3	4	4	4	4	4	3	4	5	3	5	72-210
Skip Kendall	5	4	4	5	3	5	4	3	4	4	4	5	5	3	4	5	4	4	75-210
Lee Westwood	3	5	4	4	3	5	3	3	4	4	3	4	4	3	4	5	3	4	68-211
Nick Price	4	4	3	4	3	5	4	3	4	4	4	4	4	3	5	4	3	4	69-211
K J Choi	4	4	4	5	3	6	4	3	4	4	4	5	5	3	5	5	3	3	74-211

Todd Hamilton was almost flawless; his 67 had no bogeys.

dropping a stroke on the home hole as his faithful gallery groaned. At 210, Montgomerie had fallen a stroke behind Woods and Scott Verplank. He was tied for ninth place with Mike Weir and Skip Kendall. The 36-hole leader, Kendall played nothing as all as he had in his round of 66 on Friday and slipped to 75.

Others high on the leaderboard after 36 holes toppled as well. Tied for fifth at the beginning of the round, Michael Campbell came in with 74 and dropped from sight, K J Choi had 74 as well and skidded from a tie for third to a tie for 12th, and Vijay Singh, for a time the best player in the game early in the year, stumbled home in 76 and plunged from a tie for fifth into oblivion.

Five of the world's seven highest ranking golfers—Els, Mickelson, Goosen, Woods, and Weir—ranged from one to five strokes behind Hamilton. Davis Love III and Kenny Perry (ranked No 12) were probably out of contention at 212, as was Singh at 214.

As the day began, Royal Troon seemed ripe for low scoring. Off at 12.40, nearly three hours before the final pairing, Justin Leonard birdied the fifth, sixth, seventh, and ninth holes and went out in 32;

Saturday Weather
Afternoon showers becoming clearer, brisk southwesterly breeze.

The storm peaked as Thomas Levet started down the first hole.

Shaun Micheel played the first five holes in three under par; Love birdied the first, second, and fourth, and Woods birdied the first two holes and barely missed a putt for an eagle on the fourth.

Then, just as Levet and Kendall teed off at 3.30, the weather turned foul. Rain clouds swept in, the wind freshened, and the temperature fell nearly 6 degrees Celsius, from 18 to 12. A cold, piercing rain swept in, turning conditions miserable. Pleasure boats that often sailed the Firth of Clyde on clear, warm days sought safe harbour rather than test their skippers' seamanship.

The wind shifted somewhat, and now once the players made the turn, they would have to fight it through the inward holes. Royal Troon on Saturday revived memories of a Saturday two years earlier at Muirfield, a day when Woods returned an 81 and Montgomerie 84. Els had escaped the worst of that day, but not now. He had reached the fourth hole by then, still with most of the course ahead of him.

Not to worry. Within half an hour the rain clouds dissipated, the

1988 Royal Lytham

Alister Low
Former Chairman,
The R&A General Committee

"It was a fantastic finish. Nick Price led by two strokes after the third round, but Seve Ballesteros returned a 65 in the last, and beat Nick by two strokes. Seve almost holed his chip from off the 18th green."

Excerpts
FROM THE Press

"On a day of swiftly changing weather conditions on the Ayrshire coast—wind and sun followed by a pelting cold rain followed by sun and more wind—Fox Point, Wisconsin native Skip Kendall relinquished his second-round lead to a pack of wolves."

—Gary D'Amato,
Milwaukee Journal Sentinel

"When the leaders were walking down the first fairway vertical spikes of rain began to spear the course, but by then the real storm was moving onto the second nine. Tiger Woods had showered Troon with four birdies in his opening seven holes and was just one shot off the lead of The Open."

—Mark Reason,
The Sunday Telegraph

"At a time when Scotland's stock in world golf is at its lowest ebb in years—with only two players in the top 100 of the world rankings, and none at all in the top 50—there have been promising signs of hope at this Open."

—Alasdair Reid, *Sunday Herald*

"South African wonder boy Trevor Immelman believes the burden of expectation is taking a heavy toll on the world's best young golfers."

—Steve Hardy, *Sunday Mirror*

"The scene is set for a final round full of intrigue at Royal Troon."

—Doug Proctor, *The Sunday Post*

After a good start, Tiger Woods "just didn't make any birdies coming home."

wind calmed, the sun shone brightly, and the temperature climbed back up again. Just another summer's day on the west coast of Scotland.

Woods, meanwhile, had made a run at the leaders, dipped to five under par for the Championship through the seventh, and for a time freshened memories of his magnificent streak of winning seven of 11 of the game's major tournaments.

Grim-faced and totally focused on the round before him, Woods stepped onto the first tee alongside Adam Scott, the young Australian who had won The Players Championship early in the year with final-hole heroics. Driving with long irons on the three shortish par-4s

Skip Kendall, with 75, did not have a birdie.

Retief Goosen was up and down, six birdies and three bogeys.

that open Royal Troon, Woods birdied both the first and second holes, the first with a putt from 12 feet and the second from four feet, both the result of precise ball-striking.

The gallery, of course, cheered his every shot, but still his smile remained hidden, prompting one individual to call out, "Don't smile, Tiger." Woods must at least have smiled inwardly when he ripped into a drive from the fourth tee and followed with a four iron to 45 feet. Two putts and he had his birdie. Three under now, he birdied the seventh, played the eighth and ninth in par, and turned for home four under par for the day, five under for 45 holes.

He would go no further, and indeed lost a stroke at the 12th, and two holes later missed a six-foot

Playing alongside Tiger Woods, Adam Scott went from 68 to 74, out of the chase.

Colin Montgomerie hit only six greens in regulation strokes and, on the second nine, hit only two fairways.

Players Below Par	17
Players At Par	14
Players Above Par	42

birdie opportunity on the 178-yard 14th that could count as another lost stroke. Back in 36, he had a very good 68, but he needed more. The second nine had been unusually cruel to Woods. In three days he had birdied only the 16th in the first round. With three bogeys, two of them on the 12th, Woods had yet to better par on the homeward nine and, rather, had played those holes in two over par. Yet, within four strokes of first place, he still had time to catch up.

Montgomerie, though, showed no sign he could regain the ground he lost with his third-round 72. He had begun the round within three strokes of the lead, but ended it five behind. It had begun, though, full of promise after two fine shots into the first green, although it won him no more than a par 4. Soon, though, his swing quickened, his drive to the third rolled into a bunker, and he bogeyed.

He struggled throughout the round, saving pars with steady putting after holding just three greens on the outward nine. He played much the same golf coming in, although he gave his gallery a laugh on the 14th, the par-3. His tee shot embedded in the sand, Monty took a

After a 2-3 finish on Friday, Barry Lane went 5-5 for his 71.

Ian Poulter wore plus fours after the first round.

"The biggest thing is that I've been missing it, or know where to miss it, and I have put the ball in the proper spot so that the up-and-downs aren't overly difficult."

—Phil Mickelson

"On a course like this, the best names are going to come to the top, and that's what is happening."

—Retief Goosen

"I looked at the leaderboards all the time, just to see who was doing what. I'm looking at how the tournament is going on. Otherwise, it would be boring on the course, just playing your own game."

—Thomas Levet

"This is one of my favourite courses in the world. I finished 10th in 1997, so I would love to have a great round and maybe squeak up there into the top 10 or 20."

—Mark Calcavecchia

"You are always trying to gain some experience. This being my first weekend in an Open Championship, I wanted to learn from it and try to post a good number."

—Paul Casey

TODD HAMILTON

The Confidence Of A Veteran

"This is a different style of golf, a style I don't mind playing"

Perhaps it was because he was already moving from late summer towards the early autumn of his career. Yet anyone following his play could tell there was an unmistakable confidence about Todd Hamilton during Saturday's third round. Patient and determined, the 38-year-old from the small American town of Oquawka, Illinois, was at ease enough after carding 67 to allow a sly hint of insouciance to shine through during his post-round chat with the media.

Having negotiated the exacting links without dropping a single shot to par, the veteran who also happens to be a rookie—after years of competing in Asia and Japan, Hamilton was playing his first full season on the USPGA Tour—was able to handle questioning from the golf writers with a self-deprecating humour. "I've played so bad for so long it's very strange to be sitting in here commenting on my golf," Hamilton admitted with a smile. "Usually when I'm commenting, it's to my wife or my kids, and it's usually in an angry tone."

There wasn't even a trace of exasperation in Hamilton's demeanour as he signed for a second successive round of four under par. "This is a different style of golf, a style I don't mind playing," he said. "I enjoy a kind of ugly golf, as I like to call it, where you can just chip and run it up on the greens. And this week for some reason I've been very relaxed. Even though I shot 71 the first day, I was very happy with how I played."

Out in 33, back in 34, and not an inch surrendered to the challenge of Royal Troon, Hamilton was well aware of the storm gathering around him. He was often looking at leaderboards, sizing up his own position and the challenge of the big guns.

A friend of Brian Watts, another American who honed his game in Asia before finishing runner-up to Mark O'Meara at Royal Birkdale in 1998, Hamilton took encouragement from the telephone call he made to his pal six years earlier on the eve of the last day of the Championship when Watts sounded remarkably upbeat. "I thought Brian was going to win," he recalled, "and he would have done if Mark hadn't putted so well."

Hamilton had been more successful than Watts. He won the order of merit on the Asian Tour in 1992, which gave him playing privileges in Japan. He won 11 tournaments in Japan, including four last year before he left to earn his player's card on the USPGA Tour. He qualified in what was his eighth attempt, and won a tournament in America earlier this year.

Fast forward to Saturday evening in Troon and Hamilton led the favourite Ernie Els by one stroke, Phil Mickelson and Retief Goosen, respectively the winner of the Masters and the US Open, by two, and Tiger Woods, the world No 1, by four. He knew what to expect. More significantly, Hamilton also knew his own game plan for the challenge to come. He had decided it would pay dividends to stay out of Royal Troon's penal bunkers. He intentionally laid up short of the bunkers, reasoning it was easier to find the green with a five iron from the fairway than with a lob wedge from beneath the lip.

"No one would have expected me to win, at least before the tournament started, and probably not too many expect it to happen tomorrow," Hamilton said. "It may not happen. But I will definitely be trying 110 percent."

—Mike Aitken

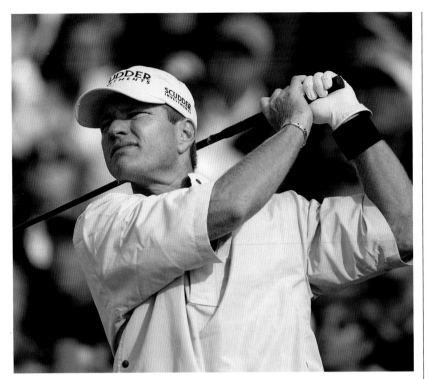

Scott Verplank was on the leaderboard until making three consecutive bogeys.

mighty swing, dug it out, and flew it onto the green. Unfortunately, he had swung so hard he lost his balance and fell backwards, but escaping the indignity of a pratfall into the sand, he settled himself on the bunker's back lip. Once again he saved his par.

Again he closed as he had the previous day, with an unsettling bogey 5, missing the green and failing to hole his first putt.

Nevertheless, he wrung as much from this round as anyone could. Usually playing his approaches from bunkers or the rough, he hit just six greens, yet one-putted 10 of them, only the fourth and seventh for birdies, the rest for pars. By now, even his more zealous supporters felt the game was up for Monty.

While Montgomerie began fading into the background, Mickelson took another step towards the fore with his 68, a score saved perhaps by a lucky incident on the 15th hole, which runs alongside a road most clearly out of bounds. With the wind coming off the Clyde towards the right, Mickelson's drive headed towards the road, but a spectator, threatened by the racing ball, couldn't dodge it quickly enough. The ball struck his leg and remained in play. Not aware of his good fortune and assuming his ball had run out of bounds, Mickelson played a provisional ball. Learning then that his ball had remained in play, he began breathing once more.

In Step With Troon's Own

By Lewine Mair

It would not have been too difficult to have guessed the main topic of conversation in shops and offices up and down Scotland's west coast on the first two days of The Open Championship—namely, Colin Montgomerie and his brace of 69s. Now it was the weekend and Montgomerie's crowd swelled accordingly, with the first yells of "Come on Monty!" starting as the player walked towards the practice range.

There were those who wondered why he was not doing more chipping than chatting around the green, but that is Montgomerie's way. He sees the range as a place to relax, his theory being that those who are still working like fury at the 11th hour can do themselves more harm than good. Judy Rankin, from the ranks of the television commentators, summed up the Montgomerie practice session by saying, lightly, "All he does is to visit with the other golfers."

"Troon's Own," was how the starter, Ivor Robson, announced the town's favourite son that day—and never mind that he was born in Glasgow and spent much of his childhood in Yorkshire before heading for university in the United States. As Montgomerie's opening shot sailed down the fairway, so his fans poured down the side of the hole, all of them only marginally less keyed up than the player himself. They were in this together, for no golfer today involves his crowd more. One moment, he will be upbraiding some unfortunate soul for a fit of coughing or sneezing, and the next, he will be doing his level best to make people feel that his birdie is theirs.

Montgomerie was starting this third round three shots adrift of Skip Kendall. He had a bit of ground to make up, and when he started par, par over arguably the easiest opening holes on The Open rota, the spectators were subdued. It had not helped that they knew, via their headsets and leaderboards, of how Tiger Woods and

Phil Mickelson had opened with two birdies apiece.

At the third, there was fresh cause for concern as Montgomerie drove into a bunker on his way to a bogey. He would drop another shot two holes later, but by the time he arrived at the turn in level par, everyone was nodding, approvingly, at the way in which this often tempestuous soul

was keeping his score together. Aside from seizing birdie chances at the fourth and seventh, he salvaged a magnificent par at the eighth, the Postage Stamp, after his tee shot had been swallowed up in a bunker on the right.

The homeward half was a study in hard-won pars, eight of them in a row. Montgomerie's 3 at the short 14th was one the galleries will remember the longest. Amid clouds of sand, the ball subsided on the putting surface while Montgomerie tumbled to ground on the back lip. At this stage of proceedings, the crowd opted for applause above laughter. It was good judgement on their part, for this was a round which was proving infinitely more trying than the two which had gone before. Everything was a struggle.

When Montgomerie mounted the 18th tee, he needed one more par for a level-par score of 71. His drive was a good one, but

his second shot failed to reach the putting surface. With the greenside crowd still giving him the equivalent of a winner's ovation as he walked up the fairway, he responded with a deft little chip which left him with much the same four-footer that he had faced at the end of his second round.

On Friday night he had missed—and now he missed again to sign off with a 72 and a somewhat anticlimactic bogey.

"I started today at second in the greens hit in regulation category, but I must have finished at the bottom of the heap after all that," Montgomerie said. He had reached only six greens in regulation strokes, after having figures of 14 and 15 for the first two rounds. "I haven't been in some of the positions I got myself in for a while." That said, he mentioned the positive side of his one-over-par tally. "Somehow," he said, "I still managed to get it round.

"It was a very good putt at the last, an exceptionally good putt, and I'm sure if you look at an action replay, it might actually go in this time. I hit it exactly where I wanted it, and how I missed, I don't know. This is still a good score, considering the way I played."

There were parallels with what had happened at Lytham in 2001. The main difference between the two years was that where, at Lytham, Montgomerie had been just one stroke behind going into the final round, he was now five strokes back. He was aware of all that but, typically, was able to recount how Justin Leonard had been precisely that far behind when he won here in 1997.

He ventured to suggest that a closing 66 could still win him the Championship.

"I do need to get off to a flying start, and I do need to be two under par after four," Montgomerie said. "If I am, the crowd will get behind me and we will see what happens from there on."

Phil Mickelson parred the last 11 holes, but it was not easy, as this shot at the 16th hit the face of the bunker and ran off the green.

Speaking of the incident later, Mickelson admitted he'd had a lucky break. "There was nothing to stop it other than a gentleman's leg," he said. "Did I thank him? Oh yeah. It should have gone out. Clearly it was a tremendous break."

By then Mickelson stood three under for the round, principally because of his blazing start, birdieing three of the first seven holes. Of course, his first drive hadn't exactly bred confidence. It darted off to the left into heavy grass, nearly into the 18th fairway.

One of his few loose shots out of the way, Mickelson pitched to eight feet and holed for the first birdie. A short approach to the second, hardly more than a chip, set up another birdie, and then a third at the seventh, at 405 yards among the shortest par-4s at Royal Troon. A big drive followed once more by nothing more than a chip to six feet and Mickelson fell to six under for 43 holes.

Playing conservative golf the rest of the way—except for that misbegotten drive on the 15th—Mickelson

While posting 69, Nick Price found three birdies—and a crow.

Round of the **Day**

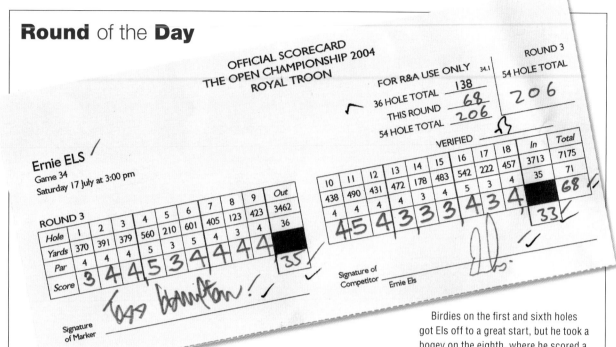

OFFICIAL SCORECARD
THE OPEN CHAMPIONSHIP 2004
ROYAL TROON

ROUND 3

FOR R&A USE ONLY   34.1

36 HOLE TOTAL   138
THIS ROUND   68
54 HOLE TOTAL   206

ROUND 3
54 HOLE TOTAL
206

Ernie ELS
Game 34
Saturday 17 July at 3:00 pm

ROUND 3

Hole	1	2	3	4	5	6	7	8	9	Out
Yards	370	391	379	560	210	601	405	123	423	3462
Par	4	4	4	5	3	5	4	3	4	36
Score	3	4	4	5	3	4	4	4	4	35

VERIFIED

	10	11	12	13	14	15	16	17	18	In	Total
	438	490	431	472	178	483	542	222	457	3713	7175
	4	4	4	4	3	4	5	3	4	35	71
	4	5	4	3	3	3	4	3	4	33	68

Signature of Marker   *Todd Hamilton!*

Signature of Competitor   Ernie Els

With six holes remaining in his round, Ernie Els had given back the two strokes he had gained in the first six and was in danger of falling out of contention. He was level par for the day, four under for the Championship, and three strokes behind his playing companion and by then the leader, Todd Hamilton.

Els reversed his fortunes with three birdies to post a 68 and finish seven under par, one stroke behind Hamilton, who would be at his side again Sunday in the final game. "It was hard work," Els said. "I had my ups and downs like everyone else on the leaderboard, but I feel good. I hit some good iron shots coming in from No 12 and got myself back in position."

Birdies on the first and sixth holes got Els off to a great start, but he took a bogey on the eighth, where he scored a hole-in-one in the first round. Another bogey came at the par-5 11th, where Els's golf ball struck the out-of-bounds wall. He was fortunate to have the ball stay in play, but he missed an eight-foot par putt. The three birdies were from seven feet after an eight iron into the 13th green, 18 feet after a nine iron into the 15th green, and two putts from 28 feet on the par-5 16th hole.

Low Scores

Low First Nine

Justin Leonard	32
Bob Estes	32
Tiger Woods	32

Low Second Nine

Ernie Els	33
Raphael Jacquelin	33

Low Round

Todd Hamilton	67

For the third time this year, Ernie Els was in position to win a major title.

Mike Weir had a 71 with two late birdies.

His 68 lifted Lee Westwood to a tie for 12th place.

For his 74, K J Choi needed a birdie at the 18th.

parred every hole coming in, some of them not easily. For example, from the rough alongside the road at the 15th, his approach rolled off the green but he still saved par, and he scratched out another par at the 16th after hitting off the face of a pot bunker. He very nearly added a fourth birdie at the 18th, but after another loose drive clanged against a metal fence and kicked away from deeper trouble, Mickelson pitched within holing distance, but, stubbornly, his putt hung on the lip.

Mickelson had climbed within two strokes of first place, new territory for him, because he had not been at his best in The Open. In 11 appearances he had missed the cut twice, finished as high as 11th only in 2000, and among the top 30 in two others.

From an albatross to an explosion of sand, Gary Evans took 6 on the par-3 14th.

But he had won the Masters earlier in 2004 and placed second in the US Open a month earlier to Goosen, who had moved into a tie with Mickelson and Levet for third place.

Levet could indeed be dangerous. To win his place in The Open, he had played the home nine at Loch Lomond in 29 and won the Barclays Scottish Open by one stroke, his entree to Royal Troon. The last man off the tee for The Open's third round, just before the heavy weather rolled in, he began by birdieing the third, fifth, and sixth. At nine under par for the Championship, he led the field by two strokes.

Out in 33, he moved safely past the 10th, but now his game turned

WHERE IS THE MAGIC?

Tiger Woods, Meet Harry Potter

More words were devoted to it than in the latest literary blockbuster

Tiger Woods and the Missing Aura of Invincibility, the subject would just not go away and there were probably more words devoted to it than contained in the latest Harry Potter blockbuster. Where was the magic? There was plenty at the US Open, but almost entirely used up in conjuring extraordinary pars.

At the first two major championships of the year, Woods failed to get the ball in the fairway off the tee on a consistent basis. His swing was off, said the television analysts, including his ex-coach, Butch Harmon. "I'm getting close," Tiger responded.

Conservative, but more consistent, Woods opened with rounds of 70 and 71 at Royal Troon. He avoided the mistakes which cost him a 7 at the 11th in the first round in 1997 and, even more damag-

ingly, 8 on the 10th in the second round and 6 on the eighth on the final day.

On Saturday, he birdied the first two holes, offering the suggestion of a repeat of his course record-equalling 64 in the third round seven years previously. He went to the turn in 32, but dropped a shot coming home and had to settle for a 68.

In mid-round there was a bit of a squall. In terms of the intensity of the rain, wind and cold, it was nothing like the storm that blew through Muirfield on the third day in 2002. But it was a poignant reminder that it was an act of God that had derailed Woods at the point that he appeared superhuman, when he had won seven of the previous 11 majors.

He was with the mere mortals now, seeking the secrets that bring a player to a peak over four days when it matters most. Phil

Mickelson and Ernie Els had stolen his mojo. While the pair, along with assorted others, assaulted the majors, Tiger was nowhere. He had a chance to win at Royal St George's, but let it slip.

With a round to play at Royal Troon, Woods was four strokes behind the lead at four under. He had never won a major when trailing going into the last day, but could he break the curse here?

"I needed a good round to give myself a chance going into Sunday," Woods said. "I was able to do that today. So now I've got a fighting chance. Hopefully, tomorrow I will play just like I did today and give myself some more looks at putts."

Has anyone got a spell for turning the clock back?

—Andy Farrell

rocky. He took three strokes to reach the 11th green, missed a 10-foot putt that could have saved his 4, and missed again from three feet. Two strokes were lost there and another on the 16th, a par-5 that yielded 23 birdies that day, second only to the fourth, with 24. Levet was one of only nine to make bogey or worse on that hole, and when he did, both Hamilton and Els swept past him and Mickelson and Goosen had caught him. Level-par 71 at the end of the day, Levet still lay within reach of the Championship.

In good position to match Woods's 2000 accomplishment of winning both the US Open and The Open Championship in the same year, Goosen played an up-and-down round, birdieing six holes and yet losing strokes on three. He scored four of his birdies on the first nine and two on the second, including a 3 on the brutally hard 11th, one of just four men to birdie that hole during the round. From the

Testing the wind here, Bob Estes returned a 69 after just surviving the cut.

Excerpts FROM THE Press

"Shank! The most dreaded word in golf ran like a shiver through the crowd surrounding the third green as Darren Clarke sent an attempted chip looping at right-angles to its target. To witnesses whose experiences with shanks are more commonplace, the sight of a top pro suffering one of golf's most freakish mis-hits was incredible."

—Peter Corrigan,
The Independent on Sunday

"Slowly, calmly and gracefully, Tiger Woods began to reassert his presence at Royal Troon in this 133rd Open Championship. Suddenly on this tempest-strewn third day the best player of his generation seemed restored to the confident expectation that has studded so much of his stellar career."

—Bill Elliott, ***The Observer***

"The earlier arrival of Masters champion Phil Mickelson and US Open champion Retief Goosen had provoked merely polite applause; make no mistake about it, this third round of The 133rd Open Championship was a home game, a movie with but one star. Only Monty's name belonged above the titles."

—John Huggan, ***Scotland on Sunday***

"If Justin Leonard has had some wonderful memories of this stretch of Scottish coastline, he will mark down yesterday as one of his worst."

—Peter Higgs, ***The Mail on Sunday***

Dropping shots on the last two holes, Kenny Perry, at 73, went over par.

Paul Casey went from 77 to 70.

Justin Leonard had 39 coming in.

The 1989 champion, Mark Calcavecchia was enjoying it.

Finishing in the rain, Vijay Singh was now six behind.

third hole through the ninth, Goosen parred only the eighth, scoring birdies on the third and fourth, losing a stroke by missing the green of the fifth, birdied the sixth, bogeyed the seventh, and birdied the ninth. He made his par 3 on the eighth.

Immediately after his birdie on the 11th, Goosen lost the stroke by missing both the fairway and green of the 12th, but he made up for it with his final birdie on the 16th.

In with his 68 and 207, Goosen headed directly to the practice ground, saying, "I have to sort out a few things. It doesn't matter how many majors you've won, it's never easy to deal with the last day."

Goosen grew up in the game competing against Els in junior competitions in South Africa, tournaments that Els usually won. With one round to go, Ernie stood a stroke ahead of Retief, at 206, following his 68, which matched Goosen's.

Els's round might have been better, but after birdieing the first and adding another at the sixth, the second of Troon's par-5s, Els ran afoul of the eighth, the Postage Stamp. In Thursday's opening round, he had holed his tee shot, but here he holed it in the right greenside bunker and bogeyed. In three rounds he had never had the same score, following his 1 with a 3 in the second round, and now a 4.

Els bogeyed the 11th as well, but only through a stroke of good luck. Headed out of bounds, his drive instead hit the stone wall running along the right side and defining Royal Troon's boundary, ricocheted into safe ground, and dropped among the gorse. Safe, although not in the best of lies, Els scrambled his way onto the green with his third shot, but missed his putt from eight feet.

Birdies at the 13th and 15th followed, and then a first-rate three iron to 30 feet set up an eagle putt on the 16th. He gave it a good run, but the ball grazed the edge of the hole and refused to fall. Another birdie, and after going out in 35, Els came back in 33, just one stroke off the lead.

"A lead right now doesn't mean much, especially a one-shot lead," Els said. "Anyone within four has really got a legitimate chance of winning tomorrow.

3

Mark O'Meara, with 68, got back to level par.

There's so much that can happen out there. I'm happy where I am."

Els would, of course, be chasing Hamilton, an unknown, although from his record, not an imposing quantity. Other than winning the Honda Classic during the USPGA Tour's 2004 swing through Florida, Hamilton had done nothing to prompt any one to expect great things. He had tied for 58th place in The Players Championship, was 40th in the Masters, and had missed the cut in the US Open.

Nevertheless, Hamilton had played consecutive rounds of 67, the best score of the third round, and led the field by one stroke with 205. He said he was comfortable playing what he called "ugly golf," meaning the pitch-and-run shots, as golf is played on a links course. "I'm usually pretty good at ugly golf, unfortunately. I enjoy this style of golf," he said.

How Hamilton did it didn't matter much, although he did save six pars after missing greens. After starting with three scrambling pars, he reached the green of the 560-yard fourth with a drive and eight iron and two-putted from 25 feet for the first of his four birdies. Two holes later, at the sixth, another par-5, he tore into a two-iron second after a 327-yard drive and

1977 Turnberry

Jock MacVicar
Daily Express

"What sets it apart from the others is that it featured two golfers—Tom Watson and Jack Nicklaus—in peak form. It was the 'Duel in the Sun' played to the death and in a wonderful spirit."

The spectators were well-prepared for the brief storm that swept through.

Round Three Hole Summary

HOLE	PAR	YARDS	EAGLES	BIRDIES	PARS	BOGEYS	D.BOGEYS	HIGHER	RANK	AVERAGE
1	4	370	0	10	49	11	3	0	7	4.10
2	4	391	0	13	46	14	0	0	13	4.01
3	4	379	0	12	49	11	1	0	13	4.01
4	5	560	0	24	44	5	0	0	18	4.74
5	3	210	0	9	51	13	0	0	10	3.06
6	5	601	0	18	46	8	1	0	15	4.89
7	4	405	0	20	44	8	1	0	16	3.86
8	3	123	0	12	45	16	0	0	10	3.06
9	4	423	0	9	53	10	1	0	12	4.04
OUT	**36**	**3462**	**0**	**127**	**427**	**96**	**7**	**0**		**35.77**
10	4	438	0	2	43	26	2	0	1	4.38
11	4	490	0	4	47	17	3	2	2	4.34
12	4	431	0	6	47	18	1	1	4	4.23
13	4	472	0	9	51	11	1	1	7	4.10
14	3	178	0	10	53	7	1	2	9	3.07
15	4	483	0	2	52	14	4	1	3	4.33
16	5	542	0	23	41	8	1	0	17	4.82
17	3	222	0	5	48	19	1	0	5	3.22
18	4	457	0	7	48	17	1	0	6	4.16
IN	**35**	**3713**	**0**	**68**	**430**	**137**	**15**	**7**		**36.66**
TOTAL	**71**	**7175**	**0**	**195**	**857**	**233**	**22**	**7**		**72.43**

left the ball short and left. There he wedged to 12 feet and holed for the 4.

Moving on to the eighth, he birdied from 20 feet, and made his last birdie on the 14th with a stunning six iron to three feet. He did not bogey a hole.

"I actually don't know what to feel," Hamilton said after he finished. "But I'm very pleased, especially the way the last two days have gone."

Els suggested the rest of the field be wary, saying, "He is a quality player who will take some beating."

It's a
Fact

Jyoti Randhawa became the first native and citizen of India to play in the third and fourth rounds of The Open Championship when Randhawa returned cards of 73 and 72 to equal the qualifying cut-off score of 145.

Jyoti Randhawa improved his position with 70 in the third round.

Fourth Round

Tough In The Clutch

By Robert Sommers

Even as his top rivals were giving it their best shots, Todd Hamilton stuck to his game plan, relying on chipping and putting to carry him to victory in a playoff.

A brisk wind swept across Royal Troon the morning of the final round of The Open Championship, threatening to raise scoring but masking even a hint of the tension and drama that lay ahead. Once over, it was clear that any one of four men could have won, but only Todd Hamilton held his game together long enough to claim the prize.

Ernie Els could have won—some will say he should have won—as well as Phil Mickelson and Thomas Levet, but each man failed at critical points.

After 72 holes, both Hamilton and Els had shot 274, 10 under par, setting up the four-hole playoff, a procedure first put into play at Royal Troon in 1989, when Mark Calcavecchia beat Greg Norman and Wayne Grady.

Calm to the end, Todd Hamilton had a short putt to win.

Hamilton won by one stroke, 15 to 16, because Els bogeyed the 17th, the 222-yard par-3, the third hole of the playoff that covered the first, second, 17th, and 18th. Furthermore, the playoff came about only because Hamilton, leading by one stroke, botched the 72nd hole. A poorly played drive set up a bogey 5 that allowed Els to catch him. With The Open his if only he could hole from 10 feet, Els missed the putt. Almost in, the ball broke sharply left and skimmed past the hole. Had it fallen, Els would have won his second Open two years after his first.

By then Mickelson had finished with one stroke too many, and the next man, Lee Westwood, who finished as the leading British player, trailed Mickelson by three.

Hamilton finished in 69, one stroke more than Els and Mickelson. Westwood returned a 67, equalling Davis Love III for the best round of the day. Westwood was fourth at 278, after starting the Championship with a double bogey, and Love tied Levet for fifth at 279.

Once again The Open Championship had been won by a somewhat obscure American with no

Holing out for eagle 2 on the 18th, Davis Love III posted a 67 to equal the lowest score of the day.

Low Scores	
Low First Nine	
Mark Calcavecchia	33
Phil Mickelson	33
Low Second Nine	
Lee Westwood	32
Low Round	
Davis Love III	67
Lee Westwood	67

great record on his home tour. Unlike Ben Curtis, though, the 2003 champion, Hamilton had already proven himself.

Hamilton had won his place in The Open field through his ranking among the world's leading 50 players and also for finishing among the top three on the Japan Tour for 2003. He had won 11 tournaments in Japan, where he played much of his career after failing to earn a place on the USPGA Tour. His situation changed late in 2003 when Hamilton, already the winner of four tournaments for the year in Japan, played his way through the qualifying process after having failed seven times previously over a span of 17 years.

He confirmed his right to play in March of 2004 by winning the Honda Classic by a stroke over Love during the tour's swing through Florida. He did it by first birdieing the 17th hole, then pitching to four feet on the final green and holing the putt. He had not only won a tournament but he had proven to himself that he could win against this company. After then, Love certainly knew of him, as well as did Els.

"Todd is such a good guy," Els said. "Whenever our paths crossed, wherever we were in the world, we always had a nice chat. I always knew he was a good player."

Lee Westwood's 67 lifted him to fourth place as the leading British player.

Fourth Round Leaders

HOLE	1	2	3	4	5	6	7	8	9	10	11	12	13	14	15	16	17	18	
PAR	4	4	4	5	3	5	4	3	4	4	4	4	4	3	4	5	3	4	TOTAL
Todd Hamilton	4	[5]	4	(4)	(2)	5	4	3	4	[5]	(3)	4	4	(2)	4	(4)	3	[5]	69-274
	4	4															3	4	15
Ernie Els	4	4	(3)	(4)	[4]	5	(3)	3	4	[6]	4	4	(3)	3	4	(4)	(2)	4	68-274
	4	4															[4]	4	16
Phil Mickelson	4	4	4	(3)	3	5	(3)	3	4	4	4	4	[5]	3	4	(4)	3	4	68-275
Lee Westwood	4	4	[5]	5	[4]	(4)	(3)	(2)	4	(3)	4	4	4	3	4	(4)	3	(3)	67-278
Davis Love III	[5]	4	(3)	(4)	3	5	4	(2)	4	4	4	4	4	3	4	5	3	(2)	67-279
Thomas Levet	4	4	4	(3)	3	5	4	[4]	4	4	4	4	4	3	[5]	5	[4]	4	72-279
Scott Verplank	4	4	4	5	3	(4)	4	3	4	[5]	4	4	4	3	4	(4)	[4]	4	71-280
Retief Goosen	[5]	4	4	(4)	3	5	4	3	[5]	4	[5]	4	4	3	4	5	3	4	73-280
Mike Weir	(3)	4	4	5	(2)	(4)	4	3	[5]	[5]	4	4	4	[5]	4	(4)	3	4	71-281
Tiger Woods	4	4	4	5	(2)	(4)	4	3	4	4	[5]	[5]	4	3	4	5	[4]	4	72-281
Darren Clarke	4	[5]	4	(4)	(2)	(4)	4	3	[5]	4	4	4	[5]	3	(3)	(4)	(2)	4	68-282
Mark Calcavecchia	[5]	(3)	(3)	(4)	3	(4)	4	3	4	4	4	(3)	4	[4]	4	5	3	4	68-282
Skip Kendall	4	4	4	(4)	3	5	4	3	4	4	4	4	4	3	[5]	[6]	3	4	72-282
Stewart Cink	4	4	4	5	3	5	(3)	3	4	(3)	[5]	4	4	3	4	(4)	3	4	69-283
Barry Lane	4	4	4	(3)	3	5	4	[4]	4	[5]	4	4	[5]	[4]	[5]	5	3	[5]	75-283

Mike Weir got within three strokes of the leaders.

Not nearly so obscure as Ben Curtis, the startling winner of the 2003 Open, Hamilton came from the same sort of background. He grew up in Oquawka, a small Illinois town of 1,500 residents that overlooks the Mississippi River. Oquawka lies almost due west of Peoria, and until Hamilton came along was known best as the burial ground of a circus elephant named, so help me, Norma Jean, the given names of Marilyn Monroe. The animal died quite unexpectedly on the town square in 1972.

Left chained to a stout tree, Norma Jean died during an electrical storm. A bolt struck her tree, the charge carried along the chain and killed her as she stood. With no way to move her, the town fathers dug a hole—a big hole—where she lay, rolled her in, and covered her with dirt. It remains the biggest event in Oquawka's history and, with the stone marker resting atop the mound, possibly the highest point in western Illinois.

Hamilton's first comment to the press after winning was, "I hope I'm now more famous than the elephant."

Scott Verplank had a steady 71 for a top-10 finish.

By winning The Open, though, Hamilton added even more glory to Oquawka, even though he was no longer a resident, opting instead to make his home in McKinney, Texas, a town north of Dallas.

Those who watched him navigate round Royal Troon understood something else about him. When he had a plan, he stuck to it, regardless of how others may have attacked the course. As an example, paired with Els for the final round, Hamilton cared not one whit that Ernie hauled out his heavy artillery on the first two shortish par-4s and whaled away with his driver. Instead, Hamilton drove with an iron, which left him miles behind Els.

His caution could have been understood on the second when Els's drive flirted with one of those pot bunkers that ambush the overly aggressive and steal precious strokes. Considering himself not much of a bunker player, Hamilton chose to play short of the trouble and rely on longer approaches. Obviously, it worked.

"He had his game plan and he stuck with it, and it worked for him," Els said. "He played wonderfully."

Thomas Levet led briefly, then fell back.

Round Four Hole Summary

HOLE	PAR	YARDS	EAGLES	BIRDIES	PARS	BOGEYS	D.BOGEYS	HIGHER	RANK	AVERAGE
1	4	370	0	8	44	18	3	0	8	4.22
2	4	391	0	7	43	23	0	0	8	4.22
3	4	379	0	7	39	23	4	0	3	4.33
4	5	560	4	25	35	8	1	0	18	4.69
5	3	210	0	6	46	20	1	0	8	3.22
6	5	601	0	12	49	11	1	0	15	5.01
7	4	405	1	19	45	7	1	0	16	3.84
8	3	123	0	5	44	20	3	1	3	3.33
9	4	423	0	3	49	21	0	0	7	4.25
OUT	36	3462	5	92	394	151	14	1		37.10
10	4	438	0	4	43	24	2	0	3	4.33
11	4	490	0	4	44	20	4	1	2	4.37
12	4	431	0	3	46	17	5	2	1	4.41
13	4	472	0	7	49	15	1	1	13	4.19
14	3	178	0	10	51	11	1	0	14	3.04
15	4	483	0	3	47	20	3	0	6	4.32
16	5	542	1	24	42	5	1	0	17	4.74
17	3	222	0	8	47	12	6	0	8	3.22
18	4	457	1	5	49	15	2	1	12	4.21
IN	35	3713	2	68	418	139	25	5		36.82
TOTAL	71	7175	7	160	812	290	39	6		73.92

Players Below Par	10
Players At Par	7
Players Above Par	56

Hamilton stated as well that his short game could be pretty good, an assessment that throughout the day he proved to be correct. "The best part of my game is the chipping and especially the putting," he said. "So I just tend to play to my strengths."

He proved it against the two most dangerous players in the game. Both Els and Mickelson had contended both in the Masters Tournament and the US Open, although Els finished with a disheartening 80 at Shinnecock Hills. In April, Els had blazed round Augusta National in 67 strokes and finished his 72 holes in 280 strokes, the apparent winner. Mickelson, though, birdied five of the last seven holes and nipped Els by one stroke, and in June Mickelson finished second to Retief Goosen in the US Open.

Both men, then, had proven they could get round the great courses in any score at all.

Behind those two lurked Goosen, Levet, who had lost a playoff to Els in the 2002 Open, Mike Weir, the 2003 Masters winner, and

Spraying shots left and right, Tiger Woods made a 72, his highest score of the week.

After a promising start, with a birdie on the fourth, Retief Goosen could progress no further, dropping to a tie for seventh.

Tiger Woods, who, most feared, might awake from hibernation at any time. Barry Lane and Colin Montgomerie entered the mix as well, along with Scott Verplank.

Refusing to fluster under the weight of other men's reputations, Hamilton outplayed them all with a calm that defied reason. Even though he fell behind Mickelson by dropping a stroke at the 10th, he simply stuck to his plan, played to avoid trouble, and depended on those strengths: solid iron play and chipping and putting. His plan led him through a rather hectic day, with first one man, then another making a move towards the front—or else simply playing spectacular shots.

Within about 10 minutes, Levet holed a chip from behind the fourth green for an eagle just before Lane holed a putt from 20 feet for another eagle. In the next pairing, Mickelson holed a chip from 40 feet for yet another eagle. Not long before their heroics, Weir had holed from a greenside bunker and birdied the fifth. Nor had it ended. Late in the day, Love holed a full-blown iron at the 18th for an eagle.

Todd Hamilton stuck to his plan, hitting irons even while being out-driven by miles.

Excerpts FROM THE Press

"The Open regularly throws up cliff-hanger endings and this one was right up there."

—David Facey, *The Sun*

"So many times you believe the script of the greatest golf tournament of them all has gone beyond its own possibilities of drama and pathos—and always you are confounded by some new extravagance, some new journey to the limits of the glory and intrigue of sport."

—James Lawton, *The Independent*

The Latin motto at Royal Troon Golf Club reads *Tam arte quam marte*, which translates "as much as by skill as by strength." Todd Hamilton, a 38-year-old rookie who wandered golf's backwaters for most of his career, lived up to the standard."

—Leonard Shapiro, *The Washington Post*

"Meanwhile Tiger Woods was doing what he had been doing all week, turning 76s into respectability."

—David Davies, *The Guardian*

Unflappable to the end, Todd Hamilton tapped in a par putt to win The Open in a playoff, bending over to get the ball as if it was just another round of golf. Then he stopped. And only then did the enormity of the moment—and how he got there—start to sink in.

—Doug Ferguson, *The Associated Press*

Once within two strokes, Barry Lane had 40 coming in.

Mark Calcavecchia made a successful return to Troon.

This had the makings of a promising day, providing the field could handle the weather. The wind bore in from the southwest at about 20 miles an hour with stronger gusts early in the day, but slacked off in the afternoon, leaving the best of the conditions to the leaders.

A number of those more than a few strokes behind made a run at them, then backed off. Woods, off half an hour ahead of Hamilton and Els, birdied both the fifth and sixth, but had no more to give. Spraying shots left or right, he played the kind of golf that would win nothing of consequence and turned in a 72, his highest score of the week.

Beginning five strokes out of first place, Weir birdied the first, holed from the bunker on the fifth, and followed with another birdie on the sixth. Six under par then, he, like Woods, had nothing left, finished with 71, and tied Woods for ninth place, at 281.

Placid as ever, Goosen birdied the fourth, but he had bogeyed the first and, try as he might, he

1, 2, 3 For Master Phil

"I thought level par on the way back would be good enough"

First at the Masters, second at the US Open, and now third at The Open Championship. As a mathematical sequence it may appear to be heading in the wrong direction, but as a body of work in the major championships it can only suggest that Phil Mickelson is here to stay. One green jacket is clearly not enough for the 34-year-old. The claret jug may not have ended up in the hands of this American at Royal Troon, but with his best-ever finish he showed it may well one day.

Mickelson played his part in the thrilling denouement, but the anticipation was almost as good. Here was a continuation of the compelling narrative created by the earlier major championships of 2004. Ernie Els, second at Augusta and in the last pairing at Shinnecock Hills, Retief Goosen, the US Open champion, and Masters champion Mickelson were all lined up immediately behind Todd Hamilton with a round to play.

"I think it is cool how we see a lot of the top players playing well and getting into contention," Mickelson said. "We are also seeing a lot of quality players that you may not have thought on Thursday would be there, and yet they are in the thick of it, too. There are a number of guys who have a great chance and it's

going to make for some exciting television."

And this was the first time Mickelson would be part of it at an Open. "Normally, I'm watching on television," he said. "I've played and I've watched the leaders tee off. It's nice to be one of the later groups."

After the 66 on Friday, Mickelson added a 68 in the third round during which he had a moment of fortune at the 15th hole. His tee shot was hooking to the right when it hit a spectator on the leg, saving the ball from going out of bounds. Teeing off alongside the man who had defeated him at Shinnecock Hills, Goosen, Mickelson began two behind Hamilton and a stroke adrift of Els.

His first move was typically dramatic, chipping in from short of the green at the fourth for an eagle. A birdie at the seventh and he was tied for the lead at the turn alongside Hamilton and Els. By the time he reached the 13th, his sequence of holes without dropping a shot had been extended to 49 holes, since the 17th on Thursday.

Two stirring par putts at the ninth and 10th had helped, but at the 13th he missed the green and failed to get up and down. At the Masters he birdied five of the last seven holes, and he conjured birdies on the second nine at Shinnecock Hills, which proved impossible for all others.

But by only picking up one more birdie at the par-5 16th, he returned another 68 and fell a stroke outside the total required to join

Hamilton and Els in the playoff. "What Todd and Ernie did was incredible," he said. "It was very difficult and I was just playing for pars. I thought level par on the way back would be good enough.

"It's disappointing, but to come back from seven strokes behind after the first day and to only drop one stroke in the last three rounds, I was proud of that. I just didn't make enough birdies to make up the ground.

"But I love this tournament. I just haven't played well in the past. I feel I've been working hard on the shots required over here and I'm looking forward to St Andrews next year."

—Andy Farrell

gained no more ground, dropped two further strokes, turned in a 73, and tumbled from a tie for third into a tie for seventh, alongside Verplank, at 280. Verplank had a 71.

Montgomerie, who had come into the round with hardly a hope, birdied the fourth, but he played the remaining holes in six over par and stumbled home in 76 to finish at 286, which was 12 strokes behind.

Meanwhile, back where the Championship was being decided, Mickelson played the first three

holes in par 4s and followed with his eagle on the fourth. Eight under now, he had tied Els and passed Hamilton, who had fallen back after misplaying the second. The Championship would be left to those three and, for a time, Levet, as one after another challenger found they couldn't keep up.

With his eagle on the fourth, Levet briefly moved into the lead at eight under, but within a few holes, both Els and Hamilton caught and then passed him as he began losing strokes. He played the first nine in 33, one under par, and the second in 37, two

Colin Montgomerie birdied the fourth but also had two bogeys and two double bogeys.

over, and with 72 and 279, tied Love for fifth place.

Off immediately before Els and Hamilton, Mickelson made that eagle on the fourth but missed a makeable birdie putt on the sixth and followed by almost driving the seventh green. Left with nothing more than a little chip-and-run, he barely missed the flagstick and holed for another birdie. At nine under par, he had tied Hamilton, who had had birdied the fifth as Els bogeyed.

Safely past the eighth, Mickelson played both the ninth and 10th like a 10-handicapper, driving into the rough twice, missing both greens, yet pulling out his pars with deft putting, especially on the ninth, where his recovery strayed so far that had he been afflicted with myopia he couldn't have seen the hole.

Playing less than a perfect round, Ernie Els had to save par at the eighth.

Excerpts FROM THE Press

"Maybe the only person who thought Todd Hamilton had a snowball's chance was Mrs. Hamilton."

—**Mike Kern,**
Philadelphia Daily News

"With shouts of 'Come on, Phil' accompanying him all the way, Mickelson would have proved a popular winner."

—**Peter Dixon,** *The Times*

"For all the bluster, all the defiant resolve, and the avalanche of goodwill, Colin Montgomerie's bid to win The Open Championship in his hometown of Troon floundered."

—**Martin Greig,** *The Herald*

"Todd Hamilton was so much of an unknown that even in his native United States the *Oakland Tribune* yesterday mistook him for Scott Hamilton, the Olympic skating gold medalist."

—**Alan Fraser,** *Daily Mail*

"His gallery had contained a group of young Scots. They serenaded him with 'Barry Lane,' a reworking of the Beatles' 'Penny Lane.' Lane liked that."

—**Mark Hodgkinson,**
The Daily Telegraph

"There has certainly been steady improvement in Lee Westwood's game since the slump of two years ago that reduced a fine game to tatters."

—**Gideon Brooks,** *Daily Express*

Phil Mickelson holed a chip from 40 feet for an eagle 3 on the fourth.

Still nine under after 11, one stroke ahead of Hamilton and two ahead of Els, Mickelson saved still another par after missing the 12th green, but now he would pay the price for his loose golf. He drove in the fairway of the 13th, but from less than 160 yards he missed the green and missed his putt as well. A bogey 5, and Mickelson dropped back to eight under. It was a mistake that cost him dearly. He would make up the lost stroke at the 16th, the shortest of Troon's par 5s, but it wouldn't be enough. He had lost The Open on the 13th. Now it was down to Els and Hamilton.

Mickelson had played wonderful golf, never losing a stroke for 49 consecutive holes. His 5 on the 13th had been his first bogey since the 17th on Thursday. Nor would he make another, a string of 55 holes with just one lost stroke.

ERNIE ELS

An Improbable Save...And Miss

Liezl had drawn a bush and ball, and her pen was poised to record what would happen

When Ernie Els took a double bogey after driving into a grassy bank on the 10th hole and then hit his tee shot knee-high up a gorse bush at the 11th, those twin mishaps appeared to mark the beginning of the end of his chance to win The Open Championship.

Els's wife, Liezl, charts her husband's progress in a sketch pad, something she has done since Harold Riley, the well-known golf artist, suggested that this was as good a way as any of keeping nerves at bay as she watched her husband playing golf in the major championships. Liezl had drawn a bush and ball, and had her pen poised to record what would happen next. Would Ernie drop out under penalty, or would he employ his forearms to give a massive thrash?

He opted for the latter, whacking the ball to the ground before hitting a glorious third shot to 12 feet. No one who had witnessed Els's drive would have bet on him making less than a 6, yet he walked away from the green with a most improbable par 4.

"It's unbelievable, the way the ball was on a branch of the gorse bush, hanging there," Els said. "It was a break, because if it goes in the bush, I've got to take a penalty drop. Somehow I got it out of there. I was quite nervous, just trying to make contact there. I made a great 4."

Buoyed by his feat at the 11th, Els went on to birdies at the 13th, 16th, and 17th to be 10 under par to Todd Hamilton's 11 under as they reached the 72nd tee.

Els had the honour at the last, and he did what he had to do to put pressure on Hamilton. He split the fairway with his drive. Hamilton sent his tee shot into the right rough, then swiped his second across the fairway to the spectator stands on the left. After receiving a free drop, Hamilton hit a pitch to 12 feet, which offered the chance for a par.

Since Els had hit an excellent second shot, 10 feet from the hole, it was Hamilton's turn to putt first. When Hamilton's putt slipped away to the left, Els had the 10-footer for a birdie to win the claret jug. His putt had neither the legs nor the line, and that gave Hamilton another chance in the playoff.

"Right now I'm thinking of the putt on the 72nd hole," said Els, when asked his reactions later in a press conference. "That's the putt I'm going to be thinking about for a while. I had such as good second shot, and it was a tough pin placement where, if you were short of the hole, you had a difficult putt.

"I didn't start the second nine the way I wanted, obviously. But I played really well coming in, and to make those putts to get back in the race was a hell of an effort. And then, I had a chance on 18, but I just couldn't get it high enough."

A dropped stroke on the 17th cost Els in the playoff. He pulled his tee shot left on the par-3 with a four iron, chipped to 12 feet, and missed the putt. "I just hit a poor putt," he said. "It was a makeable putt."

—Lewine Mair

Els fell into periodic bouts of wild driving as well. He yanked his drive so far left on the third hole it nearly carried into a television compound. Instead, his ball banged against a fence and dropped so close to it he took relief from an immovable obstruction, pitched on, holed the birdie putt, and caught Levet. Eight under par now, Els birdied the fourth, and at nine under became the clear leader.

Still, Els hadn't shaken loose from Hamilton. Relying on his ground game, Hamilton birdied the fourth as well. Short of the green with his second, he played a running shot that died within four or five feet of the hole. At no time did the putt look as if it might miss.

Now Hamilton passed Els on the fifth. Els missed the green with his tee shot, chipped on and missed from four feet, while Hamilton barely carried the frontal bunker and holed from six feet for the 2. Hamilton had picked up two strokes and moved into a tie with Mickelson at nine under par while Els fell a stroke behind.

On and on they struggled, neither giving ground until the 10th, where both men stumbled, Els losing two strokes, Hamilton one. Playing his three wood, Ernie pushed his drive into grass so heavy he could do no more than chop it out to where he could play a decent shot. Two more strokes and he reached the green with his fourth, then missed

Championship Hole Summary

HOLE	PAR	YARDS	EAGLES	BIRDIES	PARS	BOGEYS	D.BOGEYS	HIGHER	RANK	AVERAGE
1	4	370	1	63	303	73	16	2	11	4.10
2	4	391	0	66	310	73	8	1	14	4.06
3	4	379	1	59	292	88	16	2	10	4.14
4	5	560	8	150	256	37	5	2	17	4.75
5	3	210	0	53	284	117	4	0	8	3.16
6	5	601	4	95	274	76	5	4	15	5.00
7	4	405	2	99	282	65	9	1	16	3.97
8	3	123	1	82	273	83	15	4	13	3.09
9	4	423	0	30	307	107	13	1	5	4.23
OUT	36	3462	17	697	2581	719	91	17		36.50
10	4	438	0	31	277	133	15	2	3	4.30
11	4	490	0	35	264	108	38	13	1	4.41
12	4	431	0	34	285	109	24	6	2	4.31
13	4	472	0	34	332	84	6	2	9	4.15
14	3	178	0	41	342	65	8	2	12	3.10
15	4	483	0	29	304	101	19	5	4	4.28
16	5	542	3	168	238	44	4	1	18	4.74
17	3	222	0	40	296	106	15	1	6	3.22
18	4	457	1	46	291	102	15	3	7	4.20
IN	35	3713	4	458	2629	852	144	35		36.71
TOTAL	71	7175	21	1155	5210	1571	235	52		73.21

His birdie on the 13th placed Els within a stroke of Hamilton.

Els stayed one back with another birdie on the 17th. Then Hamilton lost a stroke after a drop on the 18th, and they were tied.

his putt. A costly 6, and Els dropped further behind, even though Hamilton bogeyed as well.

Now Els played a remarkable hole. As it had on the 10th, Ernie's drive headed right, towards the gorse, which is indeed where it landed. Certain he would find his ball unplayable, Els wasn't quite sure what to think when spotters led him to it. There it sat, suspended about waist high in the bush, but playable.

Els drew an iron, took a baseball swing and knocked it out, ripped into an iron, flew it onto the green, 12 feet from the hole, and ran in the putt for perhaps the most amazing par of the week. It saved his skin, because Hamilton's drive had placed him in prime position, and from about 175 yards he reached the green with his second and holed from 10 feet for another birdie.

Now Hamilton and Mickelson were tied at nine under, Els lagged two strokes behind, and the holes were running out.

Then Mickelson stumbled on the 13th, Els birdied, and one hole later Hamilton climbed two strokes ahead once more by chipping in from behind the 14th green.

Round of the Day

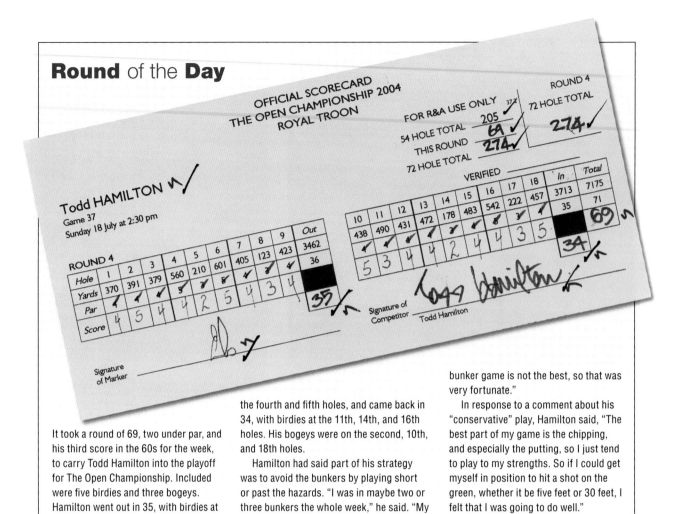

It took a round of 69, two under par, and his third score in the 60s for the week, to carry Todd Hamilton into the playoff for The Open Championship. Included were five birdies and three bogeys. Hamilton went out in 35, with birdies at the fourth and fifth holes, and came back in 34, with birdies at the 11th, 14th, and 16th holes. His bogeys were on the second, 10th, and 18th holes.

Hamilton had said part of his strategy was to avoid the bunkers by playing short or past the hazards. "I was in maybe two or three bunkers the whole week," he said. "My bunker game is not the best, so that was very fortunate."

In response to a comment about his "conservative" play, Hamilton said, "The best part of my game is the chipping, and especially the putting, so I just tend to play to my strengths. So if I could get myself in position to hit a shot on the green, whether it be five feet or 30 feet, I felt that I was going to do well."

Championship Totals	
Rounds Below Par	94
Rounds At Par	55
Rounds Above Par	309

Both men birdied the 16th, as expected, and Els birdied the 17th as well, going to 10 under and passing Mickelson, who had birdied the 16th earlier. One hole to go and Hamilton led Els by one stroke.

It vanished when Hamilton misplayed the home hole. Going with his two iron once more, Hamilton pushed his drive into high grass along the right, yanked his second sharply left and across the fairway, made the green with his third, missed the putt, and fell into a tie with Els at 10 under par.

Both had played the 72 holes in 274 strokes under continuing tension, often struggling from behind, and held their composure. Both Els and Mickelson, third at 275, had gone round Royal Troon in 68 strokes, and Hamilton in 69. Now The Open would he determined in a playoff by Hamilton's and Els's total scores over the first, second, 17th, and 18th holes.

Both men played the first two holes in par 4s, but then Els made

Hamilton struck a brilliant pitch-and-run shot with his "hybrid club" from 30 yards to within close putting range.

his fatal mistake. He pulled his tee shot left of the 17th, pitched to 12 feet, and missed the putt. He was one stroke behind with only the 18th left.

Once more Els played the home hole in classic style—a drive into good position in the fairway followed by a useful pitch that gave him another birdie opening, though not as promising as he'd had on the 72nd.

Hamilton's drive caught the fairway as well, but his approach pulled up about 30 yards short of the green. Once more Els looked the likely winner, but now Hamilton played perhaps the most remarkable shot of the week.

Taking that hybrid part wood, part iron (previously described on page 59), Hamilton played a putting stroke. The ball rolled along the fairway, onto the green, and while the gallery held its breath, turned slightly left and stopped within two feet of the hole, an extraordinary example of touch and control. Hamilton had said earlier he had good hands; here he confirmed it.

1966 Muirfield

Norman Mair
Scotland on Sunday

"My favourite was Muirfield in 1966 when the greatest player in the world, Jack Nicklaus, came to the last requiring a par out of a nasty crosswind to win. He made it with a beautiful 4, perfectly played both tactically and technically."

Hamilton Withstands A Rigorous Test

By John Hopkins

It is interesting to consider where Todd Hamilton stands in the scheme of things after his victory. What position does the new Open champion occupy in the game?

He has won the same number of major championships as Shaun Micheel (2003 USPGA), Ben Curtis (2003 Open), and Rich Beem (2002 USPGA) as well as Ian Woosnam (1991 Masters), Fred Couples (1992 Masters), Orville Moody (1969 US Open), Jerry Pate (1976 US Open), Larry Mize (1986 Masters), Bill Rogers (1981 Open), Justin Leonard (1997 Open), and David Duval (2001 Open).

Hal Sutton, the captain of the 2004 US Ryder Cup team, has one major title to his name (1983 USPGA), as so do Dave Marr (1965 USPGA), Dave Stockton (1970 USPGA), and Lanny Wadkins (1977 USPGA), who, like Sutton, were captains of US Ryder Cup teams. Phil Mickelson (2004 Masters) and Mike Weir (2003 Masters) also each have one major championship to their name.

Hamilton is one of the growing group of players who have won one major championship in recent times and by doing so raise a question. How is it that Hamilton, who was ranked 56th in the world when he arrived at Royal Troon, can triumph over so many players who are better placed in the rankings? In this Hamilton is following the recent example of Curtis (ranked 396th when he won), Micheel (169th), and Beem (73rd).

Modern technology is reducing the level of skill that was once the most important yardstick by which players were judged. "Historically, The Open is studded with multiple winners, but the last we had was Greg Norman in 1993," said Peter Dawson, Chief Executive of The R&A.

"More people are putting in the work necessary to become good players, and technology also has something to do with it. Large-headed drivers are easier to hit, the ball goes farther, it spins less, therefore it slices and hooks less. Players believe that the gap used to be wider with the old equipment."

Dawson revealed that Tiger Woods, Ernie Els, Charles Howell III, and Paul Casey had all expressed their concern to him in recent months. "I think this is the first time players at the top of the game have said that something needs to be done," Dawson said. "Usually it is the people whose powers are waning and therefore have an agenda.

"Something needs to be done and it will be done in conjunction with the ball and equipment manufacturers. The manufacturers are integral to this. This is not warfare. Everyone must have the interest of the game at heart. We will only have one shot at this."

There is a danger of damning Hamilton with faint praise here by implying he was a player who got lucky when it mattered and whose victory was due in large part to the advances of modern technology. This seems to be overlooking what Hamilton did.

In only his fifth major championship, Hamilton took a one-stroke lead after 54 holes, slept on his lead, and then came out on Sunday and went shoulder to shoulder with Els, described by Severiano Ballesteros as the best player in the world at the moment, for 22 holes and beat him. Woods, Mickelson, and Retief Goosen, whose combined positions in the Official World Golf Ranking total less than nine, all failed to make any impression on Hamilton.

This was a victory unlike Curtis's the previous year when Curtis dropped four strokes in his last seven holes. It was not won with a miracle stroke such as Shaun Micheel's seven iron. It is, in short, hard to praise it enough.

"It was as rigorous an Open as I can remember," Dawson said. "The winner was rigorously tested by being paired with Ernie Els, arguably the best player in the world, and with Phil Mickelson breathing down his neck, and he withstood them both. He is a very cool and calm customer, extremely polite and well-mannered, and he seemed truly grateful at being able to win The Open."

Hamilton's success is hardly likely to go to his head. Born on 18 October 1965, he had to endure years of trying before he achieved any success as a professional, let alone becoming Open champion. He had to try five times before he earned the right to compete in Japan, and it was only on his eighth attempt that he won the right to play on the USPGA Tour.

For years Hamilton competed in such places as Pakistan, India, Canada, South Korea, Thailand, and Singapore, and perhaps it was because of all this experience, not to mention the considerable success he had in Japan among other countries, that enabled him to stand firm on Sunday afternoon.

Hamilton is not just a big man physically; he appears to have the heart of a lion. He is a singular man who created a rousing end to a singular Championship and it seems unlikely that we have seen the last of him.

After the pitch-and-run, only two feet separated Hamilton from victory in the playoff for The Open Championship.

As he had earlier, Els missed the putt, this one from 12 feet, walked off the back of the green, and stood stoically, arms folded across his chest, watching Hamilton hole the putt that won The Open Championship.

All through the day Hamilton had shown no emotion, simply concentrated on the job at hand and let nothing rattle him, even when he fell two strokes behind. When that final putt fell, he raised his arms and whooped, then leaped into the arms of his caddie.

For Els, this had been another bitter loss, his second of the year in a major championship by a single stroke. It had also been his sixth second-place finish in those tournaments that matter most.

"I was in a similar position in April, and I played well that time. And I felt I played well this time," Els said. "But I didn't quite play the playoff good enough. I just couldn't get the right read on the putts. So I had my chances and I've got to give a lot of credit to Todd. He hung in there, and he played really awesome."

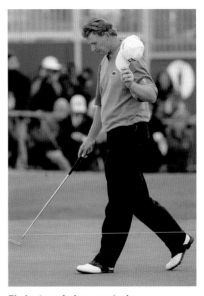

Els lost again by one stroke.

Hamilton, though, had come into The Open with no expectations at all of what lay ahead. And now, at age 38, he could look forward to playing in this great old championship for the next 27 years.

"I knew I was a decent golfer. I knew I tried hard. I knew I worked hard," Hamilton reflected. "Sometimes I think what kept me back was that I put a lot of pressure on myself to do well, and a lot of times in tournaments like this, if I happened to get in, I didn't really feel that I belonged. So maybe all that can change now."

The Open Championship Results

Year	Champion	Score	Margin	Runners-up	Venue
1860	Willie Park Snr	174	2	Tom Morris Snr	Prestwick
1861	Tom Morris Snr	163	4	Willie Park Snr	Prestwick
1862	Tom Morris Snr	163	13	Willie Park Snr	Prestwick
1863	Willie Park Snr	168	2	Tom Morris Snr	Prestwick
1864	Tom Morris Snr	167	2	Andrew Strath	Prestwick
1865	Andrew Strath	162	2	Willie Park Snr	Prestwick
1866	Willie Park Snr	169	2	David Park	Prestwick
1867	Tom Morris Snr	170	2	Willie Park Snr	Prestwick
1868	Tom Morris Jnr	154	3	Tom Morris Snr	Prestwick
1869	Tom Morris Jnr	157	11	Bob Kirk	Prestwick
1870	Tom Morris Jnr	149	12	Bob Kirk, David Strath	Prestwick
1871	*No Competition*				
1872	Tom Morris Jnr	166	3	David Strath	Prestwick
1873	Tom Kidd	179	1	Jamie Anderson	St Andrews
1874	Mungo Park	159	2	Tom Morris Jnr	Musselburgh
1875	Willie Park Snr	166	2	Bob Martin	Prestwick
1876	Bob Martin	176	—	David Strath	St Andrews
	(Martin was awarded the title when Strath refused to play-off)				
1877	Jamie Anderson	160	2	Bob Pringle	Musselburgh
1878	Jamie Anderson	157	2	Bob Kirk	Prestwick
1879	Jamie Anderson	169	3	James Allan, Andrew Kirkaldy	St Andrews
1880	Bob Ferguson	162	5	Peter Paxton	Musselburgh
1881	Bob Ferguson	170	3	Jamie Anderson	Prestwick
1882	Bob Ferguson	171	3	Willie Fernie	St Andrews
1883	Willie Fernie	158	Playoff	Bob Ferguson	Musselburgh
1884	Jack Simpson	160	4	Douglas Rolland, Willie Fernie	Prestwick
1885	Bob Martin	171	1	Archie Simpson	St Andrews
1886	David Brown	157	2	Willie Campbell	Musselburgh
1887	Willie Park Jnr	161	1	Bob Martin	Prestwick
1888	Jack Burns	171	1	David Anderson Jnr, Ben Sayers	St Andrews
1889	Willie Park Jnr	155	Playoff	Andrew Kirkaldy	Musselburgh
1890	*John Ball Jnr	164	3	Willie Fernie, Archie Simpson	Prestwick
1891	Hugh Kirkaldy	166	2	Willie Fernie, Andrew Kirkaldy	St Andrews

(From 1892 the competition was extended to 72 holes)

Year	Champion	Score	Margin	Runners-up	Venue
1892	*Harold Hilton	305	3	*John Ball Jnr, Hugh Kirkaldy, Sandy Herd	Muirfield

Ernie Els (2002)

Tom Lehman (1996)

Sandy Lyle (1985)

Year	Champion	Score	Margin	Runners-up	Venue
1893	Willie Auchterlonie	322	2	*John Laidlay	Prestwick
1894	J.H. Taylor	326	5	Douglas Rolland	Sandwich
1895	J.H. Taylor	322	4	Sandy Herd	St Andrews
1896	Harry Vardon	316	Playoff	J.H. Taylor	Muirfield
1897	*Harold Hilton	314	1	James Braid	Hoylake
1898	Harry Vardon	307	1	Willie Park Jnr	Prestwick
1899	Harry Vardon	310	5	Jack White	Sandwich
1900	J.H. Taylor	309	8	Harry Vardon	St Andrews
1901	James Braid	309	3	Harry Vardon	Muirfield
1902	Sandy Herd	307	1	Harry Vardon, James Braid	Hoylake
1903	Harry Vardon	300	6	Tom Vardon	Prestwick
1904	Jack White	296	1	James Braid, J.H. Taylor	Sandwich
1905	James Braid	318	5	J.H. Taylor, Rowland Jones	St Andrews
1906	James Braid	300	4	J.H. Taylor	Muirfield
1907	Arnaud Massy	312	2	J.H. Taylor	Hoylake
1908	James Braid	291	8	Tom Ball	Prestwick
1909	J.H. Taylor	295	6	James Braid, Tom Ball	Deal
1910	James Braid	299	4	Sandy Herd	St Andrews
1911	Harry Vardon	303	Playoff	Arnaud Massy	Sandwich
1912	Ted Ray	295	4	Harry Vardon	Muirfield
1913	J.H. Taylor	304	8	Ted Ray	Hoylake
1914	Harry Vardon	306	3	J.H. Taylor	Prestwick
1915-1919 *No Championship*					
1920	George Duncan	303	2	Sandy Herd	Deal
1921	Jock Hutchison	296	Playoff	*Roger Wethered	St Andrews
1922	Walter Hagen	300	1	George Duncan, Jim Barnes	Sandwich
1923	Arthur G. Havers	295	1	Walter Hagen	Troon
1924	Walter Hagen	301	1	Ernest Whitcombe	Hoylake
1925	Jim Barnes	300	1	Archie Compston, Ted Ray	Prestwick
1926	*Robert T. Jones Jnr	291	2	Al Watrous	Royal Lytham
1927	*Robert T. Jones Jnr	285	6	Aubrey Boomer, Fred Robson	St Andrews
1928	Walter Hagen	292	2	Gene Sarazen	Sandwich
1929	Walter Hagen	292	6	John Farrell	Muirfield
1930	*Robert T. Jones Jnr	291	2	Leo Diegel, Macdonald Smith	Hoylake

Justin Leonard (1997)

Tiger Woods (2000)

Year	Champion	Score	Margin	Runners-up	Venue
1931	Tommy Armour	296	1	Jose Jurado	Carnoustie
1932	Gene Sarazen	283	5	Macdonald Smith	Prince's
1933	Densmore Shute	292	Playoff	Craig Wood	St Andrews
1934	Henry Cotton	283	5	Sid Brews	Sandwich
1935	Alf Perry	283	4	Alf Padgham	Muirfield
1936	Alf Padgham	287	1	Jimmy Adams	Hoylake
1937	Henry Cotton	290	2	Reg Whitcombe	Carnoustie
1938	Reg Whitcombe	295	2	Jimmy Adams	Sandwich
1939	Richard Burton	290	2	Johnny Bulla	St Andrews
1940-1945 No Championship					
1946	Sam Snead	290	4	Bobby Locke, Johnny Bulla	St Andrews
1947	Fred Daly	293	1	Reg Horne, *Frank Stranahan	Hoylake
1948	Henry Cotton	284	5	Fred Daly	Muirfield
1949	Bobby Locke	283	Playoff	Harry Bradshaw	Sandwich
1950	Bobby Locke	279	2	Roberto de Vicenzo	Troon
1951	Max Faulkner	285	2	Tony Cerda	Royal Portrush
1952	Bobby Locke	287	1	Peter Thomson	Royal Lytham
1953	Ben Hogan	282	4	*Frank Stranahan, Dai Rees, Peter Thomson, Tony Cerda	Carnoustie
1954	Peter Thomson	283	1	Sid Scott, Dai Rees, Bobby Locke	Royal Birkdale
1955	Peter Thomson	281	2	Johnny Fallon	St Andrews
1956	Peter Thomson	286	3	Flory van Donck	Hoylake
1957	Bobby Locke	279	3	Peter Thomson	St Andrews
1958	Peter Thomson	278	Playoff	David Thomas	Royal Lytham
1959	Gary Player	284	2	Flory van Donck, Fred Bullock	Muirfield
1960	Kel Nagle	278	1	Arnold Palmer	St Andrews
1961	Arnold Palmer	284	1	Dai Rees	Royal Birkdale
1962	Arnold Palmer	276	6	Kel Nagle	Troon
1963	Bob Charles	277	Playoff	Phil Rodgers	Royal Lytham
1964	Tony Lema	279	5	Jack Nicklaus	St Andrews
1965	Peter Thomson	285	2	Christy O'Connor, Brian Huggett	Royal Birkdale
1966	Jack Nicklaus	282	1	David Thomas, Doug Sanders	Muirfield
1967	Roberto de Vicenzo	278	2	Jack Nicklaus	Hoylake
1968	Gary Player	289	2	Jack Nicklaus, Bob Charles	Carnoustie
1969	Tony Jacklin	280	2	Bob Charles	Royal Lytham
1970	Jack Nicklaus	283	Playoff	Doug Sanders	St Andrews

Year	Champion	Score	Margin	Runners-up	Venue
1971	Lee Trevino	278	1	Lu Liang Huan	Royal Birkdale
1972	Lee Trevino	278	1	Jack Nicklaus	Muirfield
1973	Tom Weiskopf	276	3	Neil Coles, Johnny Miller	Troon
1974	Gary Player	282	4	Peter Oosterhuis	Royal Lytham
1975	Tom Watson	279	Playoff	Jack Newton	Carnoustie
1976	Johnny Miller	279	6	Jack Nicklaus, Severiano Ballesteros	Royal Birkdale
1977	Tom Watson	268	1	Jack Nicklaus	Turnberry
1978	Jack Nicklaus	281	2	Simon Owen, Ben Crenshaw, Raymond Floyd, Tom Kite	St Andrews
1979	Severiano Ballesteros	283	3	Jack Nicklaus, Ben Crenshaw	Royal Lytham
1980	Tom Watson	271	4	Lee Trevino	Muirfield
1981	Bill Rogers	276	4	Bernhard Langer	Sandwich
1982	Tom Watson	284	1	Peter Oosterhuis, Nick Price	Royal Troon
1983	Tom Watson	275	1	Hale Irwin, Andy Bean	Royal Birkdale
1984	Severiano Ballesteros	276	2	Bernhard Langer, Tom Watson	St Andrews
1985	Sandy Lyle	282	1	Payne Stewart	Sandwich
1986	Greg Norman	280	5	Gordon J. Brand	Turnberry
1987	Nick Faldo	279	1	Rodger Davis, Paul Azinger	Muirfield
1988	Severiano Ballesteros	273	2	Nick Price	Royal Lytham
1989	Mark Calcavecchia	275	Playoff	Greg Norman, Wayne Grady	Royal Troon
1990	Nick Faldo	270	5	Mark McNulty, Payne Stewart	St Andrews
1991	Ian Baker-Finch	272	2	Mike Harwood	Royal Birkdale
1992	Nick Faldo	272	1	John Cook	Muirfield
1993	Greg Norman	267	2	Nick Faldo	Sandwich
1994	Nick Price	268	1	Jesper Parnevik	Turnberry
1995	John Daly	282	Playoff	Costantino Rocca	St Andrews
1996	Tom Lehman	271	2	Mark McCumber, Ernie Els	Royal Lytham
1997	Justin Leonard	272	3	Jesper Parnevik, Darren Clarke	Royal Troon
1998	Mark O'Meara	280	Playoff	Brian Watts	Royal Birkdale
1999	Paul Lawrie	290	Playoff	Justin Leonard, Jean Van de Velde	Carnoustie
2000	Tiger Woods	269	8	Ernie Els, Thomas Bjorn	St Andrews
2001	David Duval	274	3	Niclas Fasth	Royal Lytham
2002	Ernie Els	278	Playoff	Thomas Levet, Stuart Appleby, Steve Elkington	Muirfield
2003	Ben Curtis	283	1	Thomas Bjorn, Vijay Singh	Sandwich
2004	Todd Hamilton	274	Playoff	Ernie Els	Royal Troon

*Denotes amateurs

John Daly (1995)

Nick Price (1994)

The Open Championship Records

Most Victories

6, Harry Vardon, 1896-98-99-1903-11-14
5, James Braid, 1901-05-06-08-10; J.H. Taylor, 1894-95-1900-09-13; Peter Thomson, 1954-55-56-58-65; Tom Watson, 1975-77-80-82-83

Most Times Runner-Up or Joint Runner-Up

7, Jack Nicklaus, 1964-67-68-72-76-77-79
6, J.H. Taylor, 1896-1904-05-06-07-14

Oldest Winner

Old Tom Morris, 46 years 99 days, 1867
Harry Vardon, 44 years 41 days, 1914
Roberto de Vicenzo, 44 years 93 days, 1967

Youngest Winner

Young Tom Morris, 17 years 5 months 8 days, 1868
Willie Auchterlonie, 21 years 24 days, 1893
Severiano Ballesteros, 22 years 3 months 12 days, 1979

Youngest and Oldest Competitor

Young Tom Morris, 14 years 4 months 4 days, 1865
Gene Sarazen, 74 years 4 months 9 days, 1976

Greg Norman (1986, 1993)

Biggest Margin of Victory

13 strokes, Old Tom Morris, 1862
12 strokes, Young Tom Morris, 1870
11 strokes, Young Tom Morris, 1869
8 strokes, J.H. Taylor, 1900 and 1913; James Braid, 1908; Tiger Woods, 2000

Lowest Winning Aggregates

267 (66, 68, 69, 64), Greg Norman, Royal St George's, 1993
268 (68, 70, 65, 65), Tom Watson, Turnberry, 1977; (69, 66, 67, 66), Nick Price, Turnberry, 1994
269 (67, 66, 67, 69), Tiger Woods, St Andrews, 2000

Lowest Aggregate in Relation to Par

269 (19 under par), Tiger Woods, St Andrews, 2000
270 (18 under par), Nick Faldo, St Andrews, 1990

Lowest Aggregates by Runner-Up

269 (68, 70, 65, 66), Jack Nicklaus, Turnberry, 1977; (69, 63, 70, 67), Nick Faldo, Royal St George's, 1993; (68, 66, 68, 67), Jesper Parnevik, Turnberry, 1994

Lowest Aggregates by an Amateur

281 (68, 72, 70, 71), Iain Pyman, Royal St George's, 1993; (75, 66, 70, 70), Tiger Woods, Royal Lytham, 1996

Lowest Individual Round

63, Mark Hayes, second round, Turnberry, 1977; Isao Aoki, third round, Muirfield, 1980; Greg Norman, second round, Turnberry, 1986; Paul Broadhurst, third round, St Andrews, 1990; Jodie Mudd, fourth round, Royal Birkdale, 1991; Nick Faldo, second round, and Payne Stewart, fourth round, Royal St George's, 1993

Lowest Individual Round by an Amateur

66, Frank Stranahan, fourth round, Troon, 1950; Tiger Woods, second round, Royal Lytham, 1996; Justin Rose, second round, Royal Birkdale, 1998

Lowest First Round

64, Craig Stadler, Royal Birkdale, 1983; Christy O'Connor Jnr., Royal St George's, 1985; Rodger Davis, Muirfield, 1987; Raymond Floyd and Steve Pate, Muirfield, 1992

Lowest Second Round

63, Mark Hayes, Turnberry, 1977; Greg Norman, Turnberry, 1986; Nick Faldo, Royal St George's, 1993

Lowest Third Round

63, Isao Aoki, Muirfield, 1980; Paul Broadhurst, St Andrews, 1990

Lowest Fourth Round

63, Jodie Mudd, Royal Birkdale, 1991; Payne Stewart, Royal St George's, 1993

Lowest First 36 Holes

130 (66, 64), Nick Faldo, Muirfield, 1992

Lowest Second 36 Holes

130 (65, 65), Tom Watson, Turnberry, 1977; (64, 66), Ian Baker-Finch, Royal Birkdale, 1991; (66, 64), Anders Forsbrand, Turnberry, 1994

Lowest Middle 36 Holes

130 (66, 64), Fuzzy Zoeller, Turnberry, 1994

Lowest First 54 Holes

198 (67, 67, 64), Tom Lehman, Royal Lytham, 1996
199 (67, 65, 67), Nick Faldo, St Andrews, 1990; (66, 64, 69), Nick Faldo, Muirfield, 1992

Lowest Final 54 Holes

199 (66, 67, 66), Nick Price, Turnberry, 1994

Lowest 9 Holes

28, Denis Durnian, first 9, Royal Birkdale, 1983
29, Peter Thomson and Tom Haliburton, first 9, Royal Lytham, 1958; Tony Jacklin, first 9, St Andrews, 1970; Bill Longmuir, first 9, Royal Lytham, 1979; David J. Russell, first 9, Royal Lytham, 1988; Ian Baker-Finch and Paul Broadhurst, first 9, St Andrews, 1990; Ian Baker-Finch, first 9, Royal Birkdale, 1991; Paul McGinley, first 9, Royal Lytham, 1996; Ernie Els, first 9, Muirfield, 2002

Successive Victories

4, Young Tom Morris, 1868-72 (no Championship in 1871).
3, Jamie Anderson, 1877-79; Bob Ferguson, 1880-82, Peter Thomson, 1954-56
2, Old Tom Morris, 1861-62; J.H. Taylor, 1894-95; Harry Vardon, 1898-99; James Braid, 1905-06; Bobby Jones, 1926-27; Walter Hagen, 1928-29; Bobby Locke, 1949-50; Arnold Palmer, 1961-62; Lee Trevino, 1971-72; Tom Watson, 1982-83

Mark O'Meara (1998)

Tom Weiskopf (1973)

Mark Calcavecchia (1989)

Ben Curtis (2003)

Victories by Amateurs

3, Bobby Jones, 1926-27-30
2, Harold Hilton, 1892-97
1, John Ball, 1890
Roger Wethered lost a playoff in 1921

Champions in First Appearance

Willie Park, Prestwick, 1860; Tom Kidd, St Andrews, 1873;
Mungo Park, Musselburgh, 1874; Harold Hilton, Muirfield,
1892; Jock Hutchison, St Andrews, 1921; Densmore Shute,
St Andrews, 1933; Ben Hogan, Carnoustie, 1953; Tony Lema,
St Andrews, 1964; Tom Watson, Carnoustie, 1975; Ben Curtis,
Sandwich, 2003

Biggest Span Between First and Last Victories

19 years, J.H. Taylor, 1894-1913
18 years, Harry Vardon, 1896-1914
15 years, Gary Player, 1959-74
14 years, Willie Park Snr, 1860-75 (no competition 1871);
Henry Cotton, 1934-48

Biggest Span Between Victories

11 years, Henry Cotton, 1937-48

Champions in Three Decades

Harry Vardon, 1896, 1903, 1911
J.H. Taylor, 1894, 1900, 1913
Gary Player, 1959, 1968, 1974

Highest Number of Top-Five Finishes

16, J.H. Taylor, Jack Nicklaus
15, Harry Vardon, James Braid

Highest Number of Rounds Under Par

61, Jack Nicklaus
49, Nick Faldo
40, Tom Watson

Highest Number of Aggregates Under Par

14, Jack Nicklaus
13, Nick Faldo

Most Consecutive Rounds Under 70

7, Ernie Els, 1993-94

Outright Leader After Every Round

Ted Ray, 1912; Bobby Jones, 1927; Gene Sarazen, 1932; Henry
Cotton, 1934; Tom Weiskopf, 1973

Leader After Every Round Including Ties

Harry Vardon, 1899 and 1903; J.H. Taylor, 1900; Lee Trevino,
1971; Gary Player, 1974

Record Leads (Since 1892)

After 18 holes:
4 strokes, James Braid, 1908; Bobby Jones, 1927; Henry
Cotton, 1934; Christy O'Connor Jnr., 1985
After 36 holes:
9 strokes, Henry Cotton, 1934
After 54 holes:
10 strokes, Henry Cotton, 1934
7 strokes, Tony Lema, 1964

Biggest Leads by Non-Champions

After 54 holes:
5 strokes, Macdonald Smith, 1925; Jean Van de Velde, 1999

Champions with Each Round Lower Than Previous One

Jack White, 1904, Sandwich, (80, 75, 72, 69)
James Braid, 1906, Muirfield, (77, 76, 74, 73)
Henry Cotton, 1937, Carnoustie, (74, 73, 72, 71)
Ben Hogan, 1953, Carnoustie, (73, 71, 70, 68)
Gary Player, 1959, Muirfield, (75, 71, 70, 68)

Champion with Four Rounds the Same

Densmore Shute, 1933, St Andrews, (73, 73, 73, 73) (excluding
the playoff)

Biggest Variation Between Rounds of a Champion

14 strokes, Henry Cotton, 1934, second round 65, fourth
round 79
11 strokes, Jack White, 1904, first round 80, fourth round 69;
Greg Norman, 1986, first round 74, second round 63, third
round 74

Paul Lawrie (1999)

Nick Faldo (1987, 1990, 1992)

Biggest Variation Between Two Rounds

20 strokes, R.G. French, 1938, second round 71, third round 91; Colin Montgomerie, 2002, second round 64, third round 84
19 strokes, R.H. Pemberton, 1938, second round 72, third round 91
18 strokes, A. Tingey Jnr., 1923, first round 94, second round 76
17 strokes, Jack Nicklaus, 1981, first round 83, second round 66; Ian Baker-Finch, 1986, first round 86, second round 69

Best Comeback by Champions

After 18 holes:
Harry Vardon, 1896, 11 strokes behind the leader
After 36 holes:
George Duncan, 1920, 13 strokes behind the leader
After 54 holes:
Paul Lawrie, 1999, 10 strokes behind the leader

Champions with Four Rounds Under 70

Greg Norman, 1993, Royal St George's, (66, 68, 69, 64); Nick Price, 1994, Turnberry, (69, 66, 67, 66); Tiger Woods, 2000, St Andrews, (67, 66, 67, 69)
Of non-champions:
Ernie Els, 1993, Royal St George's, (68, 69, 69, 68); Jesper Parnevik, 1994, Turnberry, (68, 66, 68, 67); Ernie Els, 2004, Royal Troon, (69, 69, 68, 68)

Best Finishing Round by a Champion

64, Greg Norman, Royal St George's, 1993
65, Tom Watson, Turnberry, 1977; Severiano Ballesteros, Royal Lytham, 1988; Justin Leonard, Royal Troon, 1997

Worst Round by a Champion Since 1939

78, Fred Daly, third round, Hoylake, 1947
76, Paul Lawrie, third round, Carnoustie, 1999

Worst Finishing Round by a Champion Since 1939

75, Sam Snead, St Andrews, 1946

Best Opening Round by a Champion

66, Peter Thomson, Royal Lytham, 1958; Nick Faldo, Muirfield, 1992; Greg Norman, Royal St George's, 1993

Biggest Recovery in 18 Holes by a Champion

George Duncan, Deal, 1920, was 13 strokes behind the leader, Abe Mitchell, after 36 holes and level after 54

Most Appearances

46, Gary Player
37, Jack Nicklaus

Most Appearances on Final Day (Since 1892)

32, Jack Nicklaus
31, Alex Herd
30, J.H. Taylor
27, Harry Vardon, James Braid
26, Peter Thomson, Gary Player, Nick Faldo
23, Dai Rees
22, Henry Cotton

Most Appearances Before First Victory

16, Nick Price, 1994
14, Mark O'Meara, 1998

Most Appearances Without a Victory

29, Dai Rees
28, Sam Torrance
27, Neil Coles

Championship with Highest Number of Rounds Under 70

148, Turnberry, 1994

Championship Since 1946 with the Fewest Rounds Under 70

St Andrews, 1946; Hoylake, 1947; Portrush, 1951; Hoylake, 1956; Carnoustie, 1968. All had only two rounds under 70.

Longest Course

Carnoustie, 1999, 7361 yards

Courses Most Often Used

St Andrews, 26; Prestwick, 24; Muirfield, 15; Sandwich, 13; Hoylake and Royal Lytham, 10; Royal Birkdale and Royal Troon, 8; Musselburgh and Carnoustie, 6; Turnberry, 3; Deal, 2; Royal Portrush and Prince's, 1

Prize Money

Year	Total	First Prize
1860	nil	nil
1863	10	nil
1864	15	6
1876	27	10
1889	22	8
1891	30.50	10
1892	100	35
1893	100	30
1910	135	50
1920	225	75
1927	275	75
1930	400	100
1931	500	100
1946	1,000	150
1949	1,500	300
1953	2,500	500
1954	3,500	750
1955	3,750	1,000
1958	4,850	1,000
1959	5,000	1,000
1960	7,000	1,250
1961	8,500	1,400
1963	8,500	1,500
1965	10,000	1,750
1966	15,000	2,100
1968	20,000	3,000
1969	30,334	4,250
1970	40,000	5,250
1971	45,000	5,500
1972	50,000	5,500
1975	75,000	7,500
1977	100,000	10,000
1978	125,000	12,500
1979	155,000	15,000
1980	200,000	25,000
1982	250,000	32,000
1983	310,000	40,000
1984	445,000	50,000
1985	530,000	65,000
1986	634,000	70,000
1987	650,000	75,000
1988	700,000	80,000
1989	750,000	80,000
1990	825,000	85,000

Year	Total	First Prize
1991	900,000	90,000
1992	950,000	95,000
1993	1,000,000	100,000
1994	1,100,000	110,000
1995	1,250,000	125,000
1996	1,400,000	200,000
1997	1,586,300	250,000

Year	Total	First Prize
1998	1,800,000	300,000
1999	2,000,000	350,000
2000	2,750,000	500,000
2001	3,300,000	600,000
2002	3,800,000	700,000
2003	3,900,000	700,000
2004	4,000,000	720,000

Attendance

Year	Total
1962	37,098
1963	24,585
1964	35,954
1965	32,927
1966	40,182
1967	29,880
1968	51,819
1969	46,001
1970	81,593
1971	70,076
1972	84,746
1973	78,810
1974	92,796
1975	85,258
1976	92,021

Year	Total
1977	87,615
1978	125,271
1979	134,501
1980	131,610
1981	111,987
1982	133,299
1983	142,892
1984	193,126
1985	141,619
1986	134,261
1987	139,189
1988	191,334
1989	160,639
1990	208,680
1991	189,435

Year	Total
1992	146,427
1993	141,000
1994	128,000
1995	180,000
1996	170,000
1997	176,000
1998	195,100
1999	157,000
2000	230,000
2001	178,000
2002	161,500
2003	183,000
2004	176,000

The 133rd Open Championship

Complete Scores

HOLE			1	2	3	4	5	6	7	8	9	10	11	12	13	14	15	16	17	18	
PAR	POSITION		4	4	4	5	3	5	4	3	4	4	4	4	3	4	3	5	3	4	TOTAL
Todd Hamilton	T40	Round 1	4	4	3	4	3	5	5	4	4	4	4	4	4	3	5	5	3	3	71
USA	T5	Round 2	3	5	4	5	3	4	2	3	4	5	4	3	4	3	4	4	3	4	67
£720,000	1	Round 3	4	4	4	4	3	4	4	2	4	4	4	4	4	2	4	5	3	4	67
		Round 4	4	5	4	4	2	5	4	3	4	5	3	4	4	2	4	4	3	5	69 -**274**
	1	Playoff	4	4															3	4	15
Ernie Els	T13	Round 1	4	4	4	4	3	5	4	1	4	4	3	4	4	3	4	5	5	4	69
£430,000	T5	Round 2	4	4	4	5	4	4	4	3	4	3	4	4	5	2	4	4	3	4	69
South Africa	2	Round 3	3	4	4	5	3	4	4	4	4	4	5	4	3	3	3	4	3	4	68
		Round 4	4	4	3	4	4	5	3	3	4	6	4	4	3	3	4	4	2	4	68 -**274**
	2	Playoff	4	4															4	4	16
Phil Mickelson	T73	Round 1	4	4	4	5	3	5	4	3	4	5	4	4	4	3	5	4	4	4	73
USA	T10	Round 2	3	4	3	4	3	4	4	3	4	4	4	4	4	3	4	4	3	4	66
£275,000	T3	Round 3	3	3	4	5	3	5	3	3	4	4	4	4	4	3	4	5	3	4	68
	3	Round 4	4	4	4	3	3	5	3	3	4	4	4	4	5	3	4	4	3	4	68 -**275**
Lee Westwood	T57	Round 1	6	3	5	4	4	4	3	2	4	4	3	5	4	3	5	6	3	4	72
England	T37	Round 2	5	3	4	5	3	4	4	3	4	4	4	4	4	3	5	5	3	4	71
£210,000	T12	Round 3	3	5	4	4	3	5	3	3	4	4	3	4	4	3	4	5	3	4	68
	4	Round 4	4	4	5	5	4	4	3	2	4	3	4	4	4	3	4	4	3	3	67 -**278**
Davis Love III	T57	Round 1	3	4	3	5	4	5	4	3	4	4	5	4	4	3	4	5	3	5	72
USA	T17	Round 2	4	4	4	4	3	5	5	3	4	4	4	4	4	2	4	4	3	4	69
£159,500	T15	Round 3	3	3	4	4	3	7	4	3	4	4	4	5	4	3	4	6	3	3	71
	T5	Round 4	5	4	3	4	3	5	4	2	4	4	4	4	4	3	4	5	3	2	67 -**279**
Thomas Levet	T1	Round 1	4	4	4	4	2	5	3	2	4	5	3	4	4	3	4	5	2	4	66
France	2	Round 2	4	4	4	3	3	5	4	3	4	4	4	5	4	3	4	5	3	4	70
£159,500	T3	Round 3	4	4	3	5	2	4	4	3	4	4	6	4	4	3	4	6	3	4	71
	T5	Round 4	4	4	4	3	3	5	4	4	4	4	4	4	4	3	5	5	4	4	72 -**279**
Scott Verplank	T13	Round 1	4	3	6	4	3	5	3	3	4	4	4	4	5	3	4	4	3	3	69
USA	T10	Round 2	4	3	4	5	3	4	4	3	4	4	4	4	4	3	4	5	4	4	70
£117,500	T9	Round 3	4	3	4	4	3	6	3	3	4	5	5	5	4	2	4	4	3	4	70
	T7	Round 4	4	4	4	5	3	4	4	3	4	5	4	4	4	3	4	4	4	4	71 -**280**
Retief Goosen	T13	Round 1	4	4	4	5	3	4	4	2	4	4	4	4	4	4	4	4	3	4	69
South Africa	T10	Round 2	4	4	4	5	3	5	3	3	4	4	4	4	4	3	4	5	3	4	70
£117,500	T3	Round 3	4	4	3	4	4	4	5	3	3	4	3	5	4	3	4	4	3	4	68
	T7	Round 4	5	4	4	4	3	5	4	3	5	4	5	4	4	3	4	5	3	4	73 -**280**

* Denotes amateurs

HOLE			1	2	3	4	5	6	7	8	9	10	11	12	13	14	15	16	17	18	
PAR	**POSITION**		4	4	4	5	3	5	4	3	4	4	4	4	4	3	4	5	3	4	**TOTAL**
Mike Weir	T40	Round 1	4	4	4	4	3	5	4	3	5	3	4	4	4	3	4	5	4	4	71
Canada	T10	Round 2	4	4	4	5	2	4	3	3	5	4	4	4	3	4	4	4	3	4	68
£89,500	T9	Round 3	5	4	4	4	3	5	3	3	4	5	5	4	4	3	5	4	3	3	71
	T9	Round 4	3	4	4	5	2	4	4	3	5	5	4	4	4	5	4	4	3	4	71 **-281**
Tiger Woods	T26	Round 1	4	3	4	5	3	4	5	2	4	4	4	5	5	3	4	4	3	4	70
USA	T17	Round 2	4	4	4	4	3	4	5	3	4	5	4	4	4	3	4	5	3	4	71
£89,500	T7	Round 3	3	3	4	4	3	5	3	3	4	4	4	5	4	3	4	5	3	4	68
	T9	Round 4	4	4	4	5	2	4	4	3	4	4	5	5	4	3	4	5	4	4	72 **-281**
Darren Clarke	T13	Round 1	4	4	4	5	3	4	3	2	4	3	4	4	5	3	4	4	3	6	69
N. Ireland	T17	Round 2	4	4	4	4	3	5	3	4	4	4	4	4	4	3	4	6	4	4	72
£69,333	T23	Round 3	4	4	5	5	3	5	3	4	4	5	5	4	3	3	4	5	3	4	73
	T11	Round 4	4	5	4	4	2	4	4	3	5	4	4	4	5	3	3	4	2	4	68 **-282**
Mark Calcavecchia	T57	Round 1	3	5	4	5	3	5	4	3	4	3	5	4	4	2	4	6	4	4	72
USA	T59	Round 2	4	4	4	6	3	5	6	3	3	4	5	4	4	3	4	5	3	3	73
£69,333	T23	Round 3	4	4	4	4	3	4	4	4	4	4	4	4	4	3	4	4	3	4	69
	T11	Round 4	5	3	3	4	3	4	4	3	4	4	4	3	4	4	4	5	3	4	68 **-282**
Skip Kendall	T13	Round 1	3	3	4	5	2	5	4	3	3	4	4	5	4	3	5	4	4	4	69
USA	1	Round 2	4	4	3	5	2	5	4	3	4	4	5	3	4	2	4	3	3	4	66
£69,333	T9	Round 3	5	4	4	5	3	5	4	3	4	4	5	5	3	4	5	4	4	4	75
	T11	Round 4	4	4	4	4	3	5	4	3	4	4	4	4	4	3	5	6	3	4	72 **-282**
Stewart Cink	T57	Round 1	4	4	4	4	2	5	4	3	4	4	6	6	4	3	4	4	3	4	72
USA	T37	Round 2	4	4	4	4	2	4	4	2	4	5	5	4	6	3	4	5	3	4	71
£56,500	T23	Round 3	4	4	4	5	2	5	4	3	3	5	4	5	3	3	4	5	4	4	71
	T14	Round 4	4	4	4	5	3	5	3	3	4	3	5	4	4	3	4	4	3	4	69 **-283**
Barry Lane	T13	Round 1	4	3	5	4	2	5	5	2	4	6	4	3	4	3	4	4	3	4	69
England	T3	Round 2	4	3	5	6	2	6	4	2	4	4	4	3	4	3	4	5	2	3	68
£56,500	6	Round 3	4	5	4	5	3	4	4	2	4	5	4	3	3	3	3	5	5	5	71
	T14	Round 4	4	4	4	3	3	5	4	4	4	5	4	4	5	4	5	5	3	5	75 **-283**
Joakim Haeggman	T13	Round 1	4	4	3	5	3	5	4	3	4	4	4	4	3	4	4	4	3	4	69
Sweden	T24	Round 2	3	4	4	5	4	4	4	7	3	4	6	4	4	3	3	5	3	3	73
£47,000	T23	Round 3	3	4	4	5	3	5	4	3	4	4	4	4	4	3	5	5	3	5	72
	T16	Round 4	4	5	5	4	3	5	2	3	4	4	4	5	4	3	4	5	2	4	70 **-284**
Justin Leonard	T26	Round 1	3	3	4	5	3	5	4	3	4	4	4	4	4	3	4	5	4	4	70
USA	T24	Round 2	4	5	5	4	4	4	4	3	4	4	4	5	4	3	4	4	4	3	72
£47,000	T20	Round 3	4	4	4	5	2	4	3	3	3	4	5	4	4	3	6	7	3	3	71
	T16	Round 4	3	4	4	4	4	5	4	3	4	4	5	4	4	4	4	5	2	4	71 **-284**
Kenny Perry	T13	Round 1	2	3	4	5	3	5	3	2	4	4	5	4	4	3	5	5	3	5	69
USA	T10	Round 2	4	4	5	4	2	6	4	5	4	5	4	4	4	2	3	4	3	3	70
£47,000	T15	Round 3	4	4	4	6	4	5	4	3	3	4	5	3	4	3	4	4	4	5	73
	T16	Round 4	3	3	5	5	3	5	4	3	5	4	4	6	4	2	4	5	3	4	72 **-284**
K J Choi	T4	Round 1	4	4	4	3	3	4	4	3	4	4	3	6	3	3	3	5	4	4	68
Korea	T3	Round 2	4	3	4	5	3	5	3	4	4	4	5	3	4	3	4	4	3	4	69
£47,000	T12	Round 3	4	4	4	5	3	6	4	3	4	4	4	5	5	3	5	5	3	3	74
	T16	Round 4	4	4	4	6	3	4	4	3	4	5	4	4	5	3	4	5	3	4	73 **-284**
Vijay Singh	T4	Round 1	4	3	3	5	4	4	4	2	4	4	4	5	4	3	4	4	3	4	68
Fiji	T5	Round 2	4	3	4	5	4	5	3	3	5	4	4	4	4	3	4	4	3	4	70
£38,100	T23	Round 3	4	4	4	5	4	6	4	2	4	5	6	6	3	3	4	5	3	4	76
	T20	Round 4	4	5	3	5	3	4	3	4	3	4	5	4	4	3	5	5	3	4	71 **-285**

HOLE			1	2	3	4	5	6	7	8	9	10	11	12	13	14	15	16	17	18	
PAR	POSITION		4	4	4	5	3	5	4	3	4	4	4	4	4	3	4	5	3	4	TOTAL
Gary Evans	T4	Round 1	4	4	4	2	3	6	4	3	4	4	4	3	4	3	4	4	4	4	68
England	T17	Round 2	4	4	6	5	4	5	4	3	4	4	3	5	4	3	4	4	3	4	73
£38,100	T23	Round 3	4	3	4	4	4	5	4	2	4	5	4	4	5	6	4	4	3	4	73
	T20	Round 4	5	4	5	4	3	5	4	3	4	5	4	3	3	3	4	5	3	4	71 **-285**
Bob Estes	T73	Round 1	4	4	4	5	3	5	3	3	5	4	5	4	4	4	4	4	3	5	73
USA	T59	Round 2	4	4	5	4	4	4	4	4	4	4	5	4	4	2	5	4	3	4	72
£38,100	T23	Round 3	4	3	3	5	2	5	4	2	4	4	6	5	4	3	4	6	2	3	69
	T20	Round 4	3	4	4	4	4	5	5	2	3	4	4	5	4	3	5	5	3	4	71 **-285**
Paul Casey	T1	Round 1	3	4	4	4	3	5	4	2	5	3	3	5	4	3	4	4	3	3	66
England	T37	Round 2	4	4	6	5	2	5	3	3	5	5	5	5	6	3	4	5	3	4	77
£38,100	T20	Round 3	5	4	4	4	2	4	4	3	5	4	3	4	4	3	4	5	3	5	70
	T20	Round 4	3	4	5	7	3	4	4	3	4	4	4	4	4	3	4	5	3	4	72 **-285**
Michael Campbell	3	Round 1	4	4	4	4	3	3	4	3	3	5	4	4	4	3	3	5	3	4	67
New Zealand	T5	Round 2	3	5	4	5	3	5	4	2	4	5	4	5	3	3	4	5	3	4	71
£38,100	T15	Round 3	4	5	4	5	3	5	4	4	4	3	4	4	4	6	4	4	3	4	74
	T20	Round 4	4	4	5	4	3	5	4	3	5	5	5	4	3	3	4	4	4	4	73 **-285**
Ian Poulter	T40	Round 1	4	4	4	4	3	4	4	3	5	4	4	4	4	4	4	4	3	5	71
England	T37	Round 2	4	5	4	5	4	5	4	3	4	5	4	4	4	2	4	5	2	4	72
£32,250	T23	Round 3	4	3	4	5	3	4	4	3	4	5	4	4	4	2	4	6	4	4	71
	T25	Round 4	5	4	5	5	4	5	3	3	4	3	4	4	4	4	3	5	3	4	72 **-286**
Colin Montgomerie	T13	Round 1	4	3	4	5	2	4	4	3	4	6	5	3	4	3	3	5	3	4	69
Scotland	T5	Round 2	3	3	5	4	3	5	4	3	5	4	4	4	4	3	3	4	3	5	69
£32,250	T9	Round 3	4	4	5	4	4	5	3	3	4	4	4	4	4	3	4	5	3	5	72
	T25	Round 4	4	4	4	4	3	5	4	3	5	5	4	4	6	3	4	5	5	4	76 **-286**
Jyoti Randhawa	T73	Round 1	4	4	4	5	3	6	3	3	4	3	4	5	3	4	5	4	3	4	73
India	T59	Round 2	3	5	4	5	2	5	3	3	3	4	4	6	4	3	4	5	4	5	72
£29,000	T41	Round 3	4	5	4	5	3	5	3	3	3	4	4	3	4	4	4	5	3	4	70
	T27	Round 4	4	5	4	5	3	4	3	3	4	5	4	5	4	3	4	5	3	4	72 **-287**
Rodney Pampling	T57	Round 1	4	4	4	3	3	5	6	3	5	4	4	5	4	4	4	3	3	3	72
Australia	T15	Round 2	3	4	4	5	4	4	4	4	4	4	4	4	4	3	3	5	2	3	68
£29,000	T23	Round 3	4	5	4	4	3	5	4	4	4	4	4	4	4	3	4	5	4	5	74
	T27	Round 4	4	5	5	5	3	5	4	3	4	4	5	4	3	3	4	5	3	4	73 **-287**
Takashi Kamiyama	T26	Round 1	4	3	5	5	3	4	5	2	4	4	4	5	3	3	4	4	3	5	70
Japan	T37	Round 2	5	4	3	5	3	5	4	3	4	5	4	4	4	3	4	5	4	4	73
£29,000	T23	Round 3	4	4	4	4	2	5	4	4	4	4	4	4	4	2	4	6	3	5	71
	T27	Round 4	3	4	4	4	3	5	4	3	5	4	3	7	4	4	5	3	3	5	73 **-287**
Shigeki Maruyama	T40	Round 1	3	4	4	4	3	7	4	3	4	5	4	5	4	3	4	4	3	3	71
Japan	T37	Round 2	4	4	4	5	3	5	3	3	4	5	5	4	4	3	5	4	3	4	72
£24,500	T51	Round 3	6	4	4	5	3	6	4	3	4	5	4	3	4	3	4	5	3	4	74
	T30	Round 4	4	5	5	5	3	5	3	3	5	4	4	4	3	3	4	4	3	4	71 **-288**
David Toms	T40	Round 1	4	4	5	4	4	5	4	2	3	4	4	5	4	3	4	4	2	6	71
USA	T24	Round 2	4	4	6	4	4	6	3	2	4	3	4	4	4	3	4	5	3	4	71
£24,500	T47	Round 3	4	4	4	5	3	6	3	4	5	5	5	3	4	3	4	4	4	4	74
	T30	Round 4	4	3	4	5	4	5	3	3	4	4	4	4	5	3	4	5	4	4	72 **-288**
Bo Van Pelt	T57	Round 1	3	6	3	4	4	5	3	3	4	5	4	3	4	3	4	7	3	4	72
USA	T37	Round 2	4	6	5	6	3	4	3	2	4	4	3	4	4	3	4	5	3	4	71
£24,500	T23	Round 3	5	3	5	4	3	5	4	2	4	5	4	4	4	2	4	4	4	5	71
	T30	Round 4	6	4	4	5	3	4	4	3	4	4	4	4	4	3	5	5	3	5	74 **-288**

HOLE		1	2	3	4	5	6	7	8	9	10	11	12	13	14	15	16	17	18	
PAR	POSITION	4	4	4	5	3	5	4	3	4	4	4	4	3	4	5	3	4	4	TOTAL
Keiichiro Fukabori	T73	Round 1	4	4	4	4	4	4	5	3	4	5	4	4	4	3	5	4	4	4	73
Japan	T53	Round 2	4	4	4	4	3	5	4	4	5	4	4	4	4	3	4	5	2	4	71
£24,500	T23	Round 3	4	4	5	4	4	4	3	3	5	4	4	4	4	3	4	4	3	4	70
	T30	Round 4	5	5	4	4	3	5	4	4	4	5	5	5	3	4	4	4	3	4	74 -**288**
Mark O'Meara	T40	Round 1	3	4	5	5	3	5	4	4	4	4	4	4	4	3	4	4	3	4	71
USA	T59	Round 2	4	4	4	4	3	4	4	3	6	4	4	5	4	3	4	5	4	5	74
£24,500	T20	Round 3	4	3	4	4	3	5	4	3	4	4	3	4	4	3	4	5	3	4	68
	T30	Round 4	5	4	4	5	3	5	4	4	4	4	4	4	4	3	5	5	3	5	75 -**288**
Nick Price	T40	Round 1	4	3	4	5	3	4	4	4	4	5	4	4	4	3	4	5	3	4	71
Zimbabwe	T24	Round 2	4	4	3	5	3	5	4	2	4	4	6	4	4	3	4	5	3	4	71
£24,500	T12	Round 3	4	4	3	4	3	5	4	3	4	4	4	4	4	3	5	4	3	4	69
	T30	Round 4	6	4	3	5	3	5	4	2	4	4	5	4	5	2	6	5	3	7	77 -**288**
Steve Lowery	T13	Round 1	4	4	4	4	3	6	4	2	4	4	5	4	4	3	4	4	2	4	69
USA	T24	Round 2	4	4	4	4	2	5	5	3	4	4	4	4	4	4	4	5	3	6	73
£18,750	T51	Round 3	4	3	4	4	3	5	4	4	4	5	5	5	6	3	4	5	4	3	75
	T36	Round 4	5	4	4	5	4	5	3	4	4	5	5	4	4	2	4	4	2	4	72 -**289**
Tjaart van der Walt	T26	Round 1	4	4	4	5	3	5	4	2	5	4	4	4	4	3	4	4	3	4	70
South Africa	T37	Round 2	4	4	4	6	3	5	4	5	4	4	4	4	4	3	4	5	2	4	73
£18,750	T41	Round 3	4	4	5	5	3	5	3	2	3	5	4	3	4	4	4	5	4	5	72
	T36	Round 4	5	3	6	4	3	5	3	3	5	4	5	4	5	2	5	4	3	5	74 -**289**
Stuart Appleby	T40	Round 1	3	3	4	5	3	5	4	3	3	6	4	4	4	3	4	5	4	4	71
Australia	T17	Round 2	4	5	4	4	3	4	4	2	4	4	5	3	4	3	4	5	3	5	70
£18,750	T23	Round 3	4	4	4	5	3	5	4	4	4	5	4	4	4	3	4	4	3	4	73
	T36	Round 4	3	4	6	5	4	5	4	4	5	5	4	4	4	3	4	4	3	4	75 -**289**
Hunter Mahan	T95	Round 1	4	4	4	5	4	5	4	3	4	4	4	4	4	2	4	5	4	6	74
USA	T37	Round 2	5	4	3	4	3	4	3	2	5	4	4	5	4	3	3	5	4	4	69
£18,750	T23	Round 3	5	4	3	5	3	4	4	3	4	4	4	4	4	3	5	4	3	5	71
	T36	Round 4	5	4	5	4	4	7	4	3	4	4	4	4	5	3	4	4	3	4	75 -**289**
Tetsuji Hiratsuka	T26	Round 1	6	4	4	3	4	6	3	2	4	4	4	4	4	3	5	4	3	3	70
Japan	T53	Round 2	4	4	3	4	3	6	3	3	5	4	3	5	5	3	7	5	3	4	74
£18,750	T23	Round 3	4	5	4	5	3	5	3	3	4	4	4	4	3	4	4	4	4	4	70
	T36	Round 4	5	4	4	4	5	6	3	4	4	5	4	4	4	3	4	6	2	5	75 -**289**
Kim Felton	T73	Round 1	5	4	4	5	4	5	3	3	4	4	4	4	4	3	4	5	4	4	73
Australia	T15	Round 2	3	4	4	4	3	4	4	2	5	3	3	5	4	3	4	4	4	4	67
£18,750	T15	Round 3	4	4	4	5	3	5	4	3	4	5	4	4	4	2	5	5	3	4	72
	T36	Round 4	5	5	5	5	3	5	4	4	4	4	4	4	4	4	4	5	4	4	77 -**289**
Charles Howell III	T114	Round 1	4	4	5	5	3	5	3	3	5	4	5	4	5	3	5	4	4	4	75
USA	T59	Round 2	3	4	3	4	4	5	4	2	5	5	4	5	4	3	4	4	3	4	70
£14,800	T51	Round 3	5	4	4	5	4	4	5	3	3	4	5	4	4	2	4	4	3	5	72
	T42	Round 4	3	5	4	4	3	5	5	3	4	4	4	5	5	2	4	5	3	5	73 -**290**
Adam Scott	T73	Round 1	4	4	5	5	3	5	4	3	4	5	3	4	5	3	4	5	3	4	73
Australia	T17	Round 2	3	4	4	4	3	5	4	3	4	4	4	4	4	2	4	4	4	4	68
£14,800	T41	Round 3	4	5	4	4	4	4	5	3	4	6	4	4	4	3	4	4	4	4	74
	T42	Round 4	4	4	5	6	4	5	4	3	4	4	5	4	4	3	4	4	3	5	75 -**290**
Kenneth Ferrie	T4	Round 1	4	4	3	5	3	4	3	2	5	4	4	4	5	3	4	5	3	3	68
England	T24	Round 2	4	5	5	5	2	5	4	3	4	5	4	4	4	3	4	5	3	5	74
£14,800	T41	Round 3	4	4	5	5	3	5	4	3	3	4	5	4	4	3	5	5	3	4	73
	T42	Round 4	4	4	5	5	4	6	4	3	5	5	3	3	4	2	4	6	3	5	75 -**290**

HOLE			1	2	3	4	5	6	7	8	9	10	11	12	13	14	15	16	17	18	
PAR	POSITION		4	4	4	5	3	5	4	3	4	4	4	4	4	3	4	5	3	4	TOTAL
Andrew Oldcorn	T73	Round 1	4	4	4	5	2	5	4	3	4	5	4	4	4	4	3	5	5	5	73
Scotland	T37	Round 2	4	4	4	5	3	6	3	2	5	4	4	4	4	3	4	4	3	4	70
£14,800	T23	Round 3	4	3	4	5	2	5	4	3	5	4	4	4	5	3	5	4	3	4	71
	T42	Round 4	4	5	5	4	3	5	3	6	4	5	4	4	5	3	5	4	3	4	76 -**290**
Trevor Immelman	T13	Round 1	4	4	4	4	2	4	5	3	4	4	4	4	4	3	4	5	3	4	69
South Africa	T37	Round 2	4	4	4	5	2	6	4	3	4	4	4	4	4	3	5	5	3	6	74
£14,800	T23	Round 3	3	5	4	4	3	4	3	4	4	5	4	4	4	3	4	5	4	4	71
	T42	Round 4	5	5	4	3	3	5	4	4	5	4	4	6	3	3	4	5	4	5	76 -**290**
Alastair Forsyth	T4	Round 1	5	4	3	5	3	3	3	2	4	4	4	5	3	3	3	5	4	5	68
Scotland	T24	Round 2	4	4	5	5	3	5	5	3	4	4	5	4	4	3	4	5	3	4	74
£11,964	T71	Round 3	4	5	4	5	3	6	4	3	4	4	4	7	7	3	4	4	3	5	79
	T47	Round 4	4	4	4	5	3	5	4	2	4	4	4	5	4	3	4	4	3	4	70 -**291**
Jerry Kelly	T114	Round 1	4	4	4	5	4	5	4	3	4	4	5	6	5	3	4	4	3	4	75
USA	T59	Round 2	5	4	4	5	3	5	3	2	4	4	4	4	4	3	4	4	4	4	70
£11,964	T60	Round 3	4	4	3	5	4	5	4	3	4	4	5	4	4	3	4	5	2	6	73
	T47	Round 4	4	4	4	5	4	6	4	3	3	4	5	4	4	3	4	5	3	4	73 -**291**
Mathias Gronberg	T26	Round 1	5	4	3	4	3	6	4	3	4	4	4	4	4	4	4	4	2	4	70
Sweden	T53	Round 2	4	4	5	5	3	5	4	3	4	4	4	5	5	3	5	5	2	4	74
£11,964	T51	Round 3	4	4	4	5	3	5	3	4	4	4	4	4	4	4	4	5	3	5	73
	T47	Round 4	4	5	3	5	3	5	4	4	4	5	4	4	4	3	4	5	2	6	74 -**291**
Miguel A Jimenez	T95	Round 1	4	4	4	5	3	5	4	2	5	4	4	4	5	3	4	6	3	5	74
Spain	T59	Round 2	4	4	4	4	3	5	4	2	5	4	4	6	3	3	4	4	3	4	71
£11,964	T47	Round 3	4	4	3	5	3	5	4	4	5	4	4	4	2	4	5	5	3	4	71
	T47	Round 4	5	4	5	4	3	5	4	4	4	4	4	5	4	4	5	4	3	4	75 -**291**
Sean Whiffin	T73	Round 1	4	4	4	5	4	5	5	3	5	4	4	3	3	3	4	5	3	4	73
England	T59	Round 2	4	4	4	5	3	5	4	2	5	5	4	6	4	3	4	4	3	3	72
£11,964	T47	Round 3	4	4	5	4	3	5	3	4	4	4	4	5	3	3	4	5	3	4	71
	T47	Round 4	4	3	4	5	4	6	3	3	4	4	6	4	4	3	4	7	3	4	75 -**291**
Paul Bradshaw	T114	Round 1	4	4	4	4	3	5	4	3	4	4	4	5	4	3	6	5	3	6	75
England	T24	Round 2	5	4	2	4	3	5	4	5	4	3	3	3	4	3	4	4	3	4	67
£11,964	T23	Round 3	3	5	4	5	3	5	3	2	4	4	4	4	4	5	5	5	4	4	72
	T47	Round 4	4	5	5	4	4	5	5	4	4	4	4	5	5	4	4	4	3	4	77 -**291**
Shaun Micheel	T26	Round 1	4	3	3	5	3	4	5	2	6	4	5	3	4	3	4	4	4	4	70
USA	T24	Round 2	4	3	4	6	2	5	4	3	4	4	4	5	4	4	4	5	3	4	72
£11,964	T15	Round 3	3	4	4	4	2	6	3	3	4	4	4	4	5	3	4	5	4	4	70
	T47	Round 4	6	5	3	5	3	5	4	3	5	4	6	5	4	3	5	6	4	3	79 -**291**
Raphael Jacquelin	T57	Round 1	4	5	4	5	3	4	4	4	4	4	4	4	5	3	3	5	3	4	72
France	T53	Round 2	5	4	4	5	3	5	5	3	4	5	5	3	4	3	3	5	2	4	72
£10,550	T51	Round 3	5	4	6	5	3	5	5	2	5	3	4	4	4	3	4	5	2	4	73
	T54	Round 4	4	4	4	6	4	5	4	3	4	4	6	4	3	3	4	5	5	3	75 -**292**
Ignacio Garrido	T40	Round 1	4	4	4	5	3	6	3	3	4	4	4	4	4	2	5	5	3	4	71
Spain	T59	Round 2	4	4	7	5	3	4	5	3	4	3	5	4	4	3	4	5	3	4	74
£10,550	T51	Round 3	4	4	3	5	2	6	4	3	4	4	4	5	5	3	4	5	3	4	72
	T54	Round 4	4	5	4	5	3	6	4	3	4	5	4	5	4	3	4	5	3	4	75 -**292**
Steve Flesch	T114	Round 1	6	3	4	4	3	7	4	3	4	4	5	4	4	4	4	4	3	5	75
USA	T59	Round 2	4	5	4	4	4	5	3	3	4	4	4	5	4	3	4	3	3	4	70
£10,550	T41	Round 3	5	4	3	6	3	4	3	3	4	4	4	4	3	3	5	5	2	5	70
	T54	Round 4	4	4	5	5	3	5	3	4	4	5	4	4	5	3	4	5	5	5	77 -**292**

HOLE			1	2	3	4	5	6	7	8	9	10	11	12	13	14	15	16	17	18	
PAR	POSITION		4	4	4	5	3	5	4	3	4	4	4	4	4	3	4	5	3	4	TOTAL
Paul McGinley	T13	Round 1	5	3	3	5	3	5	4	3	4	4	4	4	4	3	4	4	3	4	69
Ireland	T59	Round 2	4	4	3	5	3	5	4	3	4	5	6	6	4	3	5	5	3	4	76
£10,200	T66	Round 3	4	4	4	5	3	5	5	3	4	4	7	4	4	2	5	4	4	4	75
	T57	Round 4	4	4	4	4	3	6	3	3	4	5	4	4	4	3	5	5	4	4	73 -**293**
Carl Pettersson	T4	Round 1	3	3	3	5	3	5	4	3	4	4	5	4	4	3	4	4	3	4	68
Sweden	T59	Round 2	5	5	3	4	2	6	5	3	6	4	4	5	5	3	5	5	3	4	77
£10,200	T62	Round 3	4	5	5	6	3	5	5	3	4	5	4	4	3	3	4	5	3	3	74
	T57	Round 4	4	5	4	4	3	6	4	3	4	4	5	5	4	3	4	5	3	4	74 -**293**
James Kingston	T73	Round 1	3	4	4	6	4	4	4	2	4	4	4	4	4	4	6	4	4	4	73
South Africa	T59	Round 2	4	5	4	5	3	5	4	3	4	4	4	5	4	3	4	4	3	4	72
£10,200	T62	Round 3	6	4	4	5	4	5	5	3	4	4	4	4	4	3	4	4	3	4	74
	T57	Round 4	4	5	4	5	3	5	4	4	4	5	4	4	4	3	5	4	3	4	74 -**293**
Gary Emerson	T26	Round 1	3	4	4	5	3	5	4	2	4	4	5	4	5	3	4	4	2	5	70
England	T17	Round 2	4	4	5	5	4	5	4	3	4	5	3	3	4	3	4	4	3	4	71
£9,900	T51	Round 3	6	4	4	5	3	5	5	3	5	4	4	5	4	3	4	4	3	5	76
	T60	Round 4	5	5	4	4	2	6	4	5	4	4	5	7	4	3	4	4	3	4	77 -**294**
Paul Broadhurst	T40	Round 1	6	3	4	4	2	4	4	3	4	4	4	5	4	3	4	5	3	5	71
England	T59	Round 2	4	5	4	5	3	4	4	3	5	4	7	4	4	3	4	4	2	5	74
£9,900	T51	Round 3	4	5	4	4	4	5	4	2	6	4	4	4	4	3	4	4	3	4	72
	T60	Round 4	4	4	5	5	2	6	4	3	4	6	3	6	5	3	5	5	2	5	77 -**294**
Brad Faxon	T95	Round 1	4	3	4	5	3	4	4	4	4	6	5	4	4	3	4	5	3	5	74
USA	T24	Round 2	4	5	5	6	3	5	3	2	4	4	3	3	3	2	4	5	3	4	68
£9,900	T41	Round 3	4	4	4	5	3	5	4	3	4	4	4	5	3	4	5	4	4	4	73
	T60	Round 4	4	5	4	5	3	5	3	3	4	5	7	6	4	4	5	6	3	3	79 -**294**
Chris DiMarco	T40	Round 1	4	3	4	4	3	5	4	4	4	4	7	4	4	3	3	5	3	3	71
USA	T24	Round 2	4	4	3	5	4	5	5	2	4	4	4	3	4	3	4	4	4	5	71
£9,650	T66	Round 3	4	4	4	5	4	5	6	2	4	5	5	4	4	3	6	6	3	4	78
	T63	Round 4	4	5	5	5	3	6	5	4	5	4	5	4	4	3	4	4	3	3	76 -**296**
***Stuart Wilson**	T4	Round 1	3	4	4	4	3	4	3	3	4	4	4	4	4	4	4	5	3	4	68
Scotland	T37	Round 2	4	4	4	5	3	5	5	3	4	3	5	4	5	4	5	5	3	4	75
	T66	Round 3	5	4	4	5	3	4	4	3	5	5	5	5	5	3	5	5	3	4	77
	T63	Round 4	4	3	6	6	3	5	4	3	5	5	5	5	4	2	4	5	3	4	76 -**296**
Mark Foster	T40	Round 1	3	4	4	4	2	5	4	7	4	4	4	4	4	3	4	4	3	4	71
England	T37	Round 2	4	4	4	5	3	5	4	3	5	4	5	5	4	3	4	4	3	3	72
£9,650	T62	Round 3	4	5	4	5	3	5	4	3	5	5	5	5	4	3	4	6	2	5	76
	T63	Round 4	4	4	5	5	4	6	5	3	4	4	4	5	4	3	5	5	3	4	77 -**296**
Marten Olander	T4	Round 1	3	4	3	5	3	5	3	3	4	4	5	4	4	3	4	4	3	4	68
Sweden	T24	Round 2	4	4	3	5	3	5	5	2	5	4	4	5	5	4	4	5	3	4	74
£9,450	T66	Round 3	4	5	3	5	3	5	4	4	4	5	5	5	4	2	8	5	3	4	78
	T66	Round 4	4	4	5	5	3	5	3	4	4	5	5	4	4	3	6	5	3	5	77 -**297**
Rory Sabbatini	T40	Round 1	3	4	3	5	3	5	4	3	5	4	4	4	5	3	4	4	3	5	71
South Africa	T37	Round 2	4	4	4	5	3	4	4	3	4	5	5	4	5	3	4	4	3	4	72
£9,450	T47	Round 3	4	4	3	4	3	5	4	3	4	5	5	4	4	4	6	3	4	73
	T66	Round 4	4	4	6	6	3	.5	3	5	5	3	4	4	5	4	5	6	5	4	81 -**297**
Paul Wesselingh	T73	Round 1	4	6	4	4	3	5	4	2	4	4	4	5	4	3	5	4	3	5	73
England	T59	Round 2	4	4	4	4	4	5	3	3	4	4	4	4	5	4	4	5	3	4	72
£9,250	T71	Round 3	5	4	5	5	4	5	4	3	3	5	4	5	4	4	4	5	3	4	76
	T68	Round 4	5	4	4	5	3	5	5	4	4	4	5	5	4	3	4	5	4	4	77 -**298**

HOLE			1	2	3	4	5	6	7	8	9	10	11	12	13	14	15	16	17	18	
PAR	POSITION		4	4	4	5	3	5	4	3	4	4	4	4	4	3	4	5	3	4	TOTAL
Martin Erlandsson	T73	Round 1	4	4	3	5	3	5	5	3	5	3	5	4	4	4	4	5	3	4	73
Sweden	T37	Round 2	5	4	3	5	2	4	4	3	4	3	5	5	4	3	4	4	4	4	70
£9,250	T66	Round 3	4	4	4	6	3	4	3	3	5	5	7	5	5	3	4	5	3	4	77
	T68	Round 4	5	3	4	6	4	4	4	4	5	4	4	6	4	3	5	5	3	5	78 -298
Bob Tway	T128	Round 1	4	4	4	5	4	5	4	3	4	5	5	4	4	3	5	5	4	4	76
USA	T53	Round 2	4	4	4	4	3	4	4	3	4	3	4	4	4	3	5	4	3	4	68
£9,100	T51	Round 3	5	4	4	5	3	5	4	2	4	4	4	4	4	3	5	5	4	4	73
	70	Round 4	4	5	5	6	4	5	4	4	5	4	4	5	5	4	4	5	5	4	82 -299
Rich Beem	T13	Round 1	3	4	4	5	3	3	4	2	3	4	5	5	4	3	4	5	4	4	69
USA	T24	Round 2	4	6	5	4	3	5	3	2	4	4	4	5	5	3	4	4	4	4	73
£8,950	T62	Round 3	3	3	5	5	3	5	4	4	5	5	5	4	5	3	5	5	4	4	77
	T71	Round 4	5	4	5	5	4	5	5	4	5	4	6	4	4	3	6	4	4	4	81 -300
Christian Cevaer	T26	Round 1	4	4	5	5	2	4	5	4	4	5	4	3	5	3	4	4	2	3	70
France	T53	Round 2	4	5	4	5	4	5	3	2	4	4	6	4	5	3	3	6	3	4	74
£8,950	T60	Round 3	4	4	3	5	3	5	4	4	4	4	5	4	4	3	6	5	3	4	74
	T71	Round 4	4	4	4	6	3	5	3	5	5	5	4	4	8	2	5	5	4	6	82 -300
Sandy Lyle	T26	Round 1	3	4	5	4	2	5	5	3	4	4	4	5	3	3	4	4	3	5	70
Scotland	T37	Round 2	5	4	4	5	3	5	5	2	4	4	3	5	4	3	4	5	4	4	73
£8,800	73	Round 3	4	4	5	6	3	4	4	3	4	6	4	5	5	4	6	5	4	5	81
	73	Round 4	4	5	4	5	5	6	4	3	5	4	5	5	4	2	4	5	5	4	79 -303

NON QUALIFIERS AFTER 36 HOLES

(Leading 10 professionals and ties receive £3,000 each, next 20 professionals and ties receive £2,500 each, next 20 professionals and ties receive £2,250 each, remainder of professionals receive £2,000 each.)

HOLE			1	2	3	4	5	6	7	8	9	10	11	12	13	14	15	16	17	18	
PAR	POSITION		4	4	4	5	3	5	4	3	4	4	4	4	4	3	4	5	3	4	TOTAL
S K Ho	T57	Round 1	4	3	4	4	3	5	4	3	4	3	5	5	5	3	4	4	4	5	72
Korea	**T74**	Round 2	5	4	3	4	3	5	5	3	4	4	4	5	4	4	4	6	3	4	74 -146
Chad Campbell	T57	Round 1	6	4	4	5	3	4	4	4	4	3	4	4	3	3	5	5	3	4	72
USA	**T74**	Round 2	4	5	3	7	3	4	3	3	4	5	4	5	4	3	4	5	4	4	74 -146
Jay Haas	T26	Round 1	4	4	4	5	3	4	3	3	4	5	4	4	4	3	4	5	3	4	70
USA	**T74**	Round 2	4	4	4	5	4	5	4	3	5	4	4	4	4	4	5	5	4	4	76 -146
Tim Clark	T73	Round 1	4	4	4	5	3	5	3	3	5	3	5	5	4	3	4	5	3	5	73
South Africa	**T74**	Round 2	4	4	5	5	3	5	4	3	4	4	4	3	4	3	4	4	5	5	73 -146
Scott Barr	T26	Round 1	4	4	4	4	3	4	4	3	4	5	4	4	4	2	4	4	4	5	70
Australia	**T74**	Round 2	4	4	5	5	2	5	3	5	5	5	5	4	5	3	4	5	3	4	76 -146
Jim Furyk	T73	Round 1	3	3	5	5	3	6	5	3	5	3	4	4	5	2	5	5	3	4	73
USA	**T74**	Round 2	3	4	5	5	3	5	5	3	4	5	4	4	5	3	4	5	3	3	73 -146
Fredrik Jacobson	T114	Round 1	4	4	5	5	3	4	8	3	4	4	6	4	4	3	4	4	2	4	75
Sweden	**T74**	Round 2	3	5	5	4	3	5	3	3	4	4	5	5	4	3	4	4	3	4	71 -146
Luke Donald	T114	Round 1	4	4	4	4	3	5	4	4	3	4	6	4	5	3	4	5	5	4	75
England	**T74**	Round 2	4	3	4	6	3	5	4	3	4	4	5	4	3	3	3	5	3	5	71 -146
Mathew Goggin	T4	Round 1	4	3	4	4	3	4	4	3	5	4	4	4	3	3	5	4	3	4	68
Australia	**T74**	Round 2	4	4	4	5	3	6	3	4	5	4	5	6	4	4	4	5	3	5	78 -146
Euan Little	T95	Round 1	4	4	4	6	4	6	4	3	5	4	4	5	3	3	3	4	3	4	74
Scotland	**T74**	Round 2	4	5	4	4	4	6	5	2	4	4	4	3	4	3	4	4	3	5	72 -146

HOLE			1	2	3	4	5	6	7	8	9	10	11	12	13	14	15	16	17	18	
PAR	POSITION		4	4	4	5	3	5	4	3	4	4	4	4	4	3	4	5	3	4	TOTAL
Klas Eriksson	T73	Round 1	4	5	4	5	2	5	4	2	4	4	5	4	4	3	4	4	4	6	73
Sweden	**T74**	Round 2	4	5	3	4	3	5	5	3	6	3	4	4	5	3	5	5	3	3	73-**146**
Peter Lonard	T128	Round 1	4	4	4	5	4	6	5	4	5	5	5	4	2	4	4	4	3	4	76
Australia	**T85**	Round 2	4	5	4	5	3	5	4	3	4	4	4	3	4	3	4	4	3	5	71-**147**
Stephen Leaney	T73	Round 1	5	4	4	4	3	6	4	3	4	4	4	4	4	3	5	4	3	5	73
Australia	**T85**	Round 2	5	4	4	5	3	5	3	4	4	4	5	4	4	3	4	5	3	5	74-**147**
Robert Allenby	T26	Round 1	4	4	4	6	3	3	4	3	5	4	4	4	2	4	4	4	3	5	70
Australia	**T85**	Round 2	4	4	3	5	3	6	4	3	5	4	4	7	4	4	5	5	3	4	77-**147**
Jonathan Cheetham	T57	Round 1	4	3	4	5	4	5	4	3	4	4	4	4	4	3	4	5	3	5	72
England	**T85**	Round 2	4	5	3	6	3	5	4	2	4	5	6	4	4	3	4	5	3	5	75-**147**
Jean F Remesy	T95	Round 1	4	4	4	7	3	5	5	2	4	4	4	3	4	3	4	6	5	3	74
France	**T85**	Round 2	4	4	5	5	2	6	5	3	3	5	4	4	4	3	4	5	3	4	73-**147**
Sven Struver	T95	Round 1	4	5	4	4	4	4	3	4	4	4	4	4	4	4	4	5	3	6	74
Germany	**T85**	Round 2	4	5	4	5	3	5	4	3	4	4	3	4	4	3	5	5	4	4	73-**147**
***Lloyd Campbell**	T73	Round 1	5	4	4	4	3	5	4	3	3	5	6	4	4	4	4	4	2	5	73
England	**T85**	Round 2	4	5	4	7	3	5	4	2	4	4	4	4	4	3	4	5	3	5	74-**147**
Grant Muller	T73	Round 1	5	3	4	5	4	5	4	3	4	4	5	4	4	3	4	4	3	5	73
South Africa	**T85**	Round 2	4	3	3	5	4	4	4	3	4	7	5	5	4	3	5	4	3	4	74-**147**
Peter O'Malley	T137	Round 1	4	4	4	6	3	5	4	3	3	5	4	5	4	3	5	4	4	7	77
Australia	**T85**	Round 2	4	4	4	4	3	5	4	3	4	3	6	4	4	3	4	4	3	4	70-**147**
Craig Parry	T128	Round 1	4	4	4	5	4	5	4	3	4	5	6	4	4	3	4	6	3	4	76
Australia	**T85**	Round 2	4	4	4	5	3	5	3	3	4	4	4	4	4	3	4	6	4	3	71-**147**
Brandan Jones	T40	Round 1	4	4	4	4	2	5	4	3	4	4	5	4	3	5	5	5	3	3	71
Australia	**T85**	Round 2	4	4	4	5	4	5	4	3	3	5	6	4	4	3	5	5	3	5	76-**147**
Chris Riley	T57	Round 1	4	4	4	4	3	4	4	4	4	5	4	4	4	5	4	5	3	3	72
USA	**T85**	Round 2	4	3	5	5	4	6	4	3	5	4	4	4	4	3	4	5	4	4	75-**147**
Paul Sheehan	T114	Round 1	5	3	3	4	3	5	4	3	4	4	4	5	5	3	4	5	7	4	75
Australia	**T85**	Round 2	4	4	3	5	3	5	5	2	5	4	5	4	5	3	4	5	2	4	72-**147**
Padraig Harrington	T128	Round 1	4	4	4	5	3	5	4	3	4	5	7	4	4	4	4	4	3	5	76
Ireland	**T85**	Round 2	4	4	4	4	2	6	3	3	4	4	3	5	4	4	4	4	4	5	71-**147**
***Steven Tiley**	T40	Round 1	5	4	4	5	3	5	4	2	5	4	4	4	4	2	4	5	3	4	71
England	**T85**	Round 2	4	4	4	5	4	5	4	4	5	4	5	4	4	3	3	5	5	4	76-**147**
Glen Day	T95	Round 1	4	4	4	6	3	5	5	3	4	5	5	4	4	3	4	4	3	4	74
USA	**T85**	Round 2	4	3	5	5	3	5	4	2	4	4	4	4	5	3	5	5	4	4	73-**147**
Barry Hume	T57	Round 1	4	4	4	5	3	5	4	3	4	5	4	5	4	3	4	4	3	4	72
Scotland	**T85**	Round 2	5	4	6	5	2	5	5	5	4	4	3	5	4	3	3	4	3	5	75-**147**
John Huston	T114	Round 1	4	4	4	5	3	6	5	3	5	4	6	4	4	3	4	6	2	3	75
USA	**T102**	Round 2	3	4	4	4	2	5	4	4	5	4	5	5	4	4	4	4	3	5	73-**148**
John Daly	T26	Round 1	4	4	4	5	3	5	4	3	4	4	3	5	4	3	4	5	2	4	70
USA	**T102**	Round 2	3	4	4	5	3	6	5	3	4	5	4	5	5	3	7	5	2	5	78-**148**
Phillip Price	T114	Round 1	4	4	4	4	3	5	6	3	4	5	6	4	4	3	5	4	3	4	75
Wales	**T102**	Round 2	4	4	4	5	3	5	4	3	3	4	5	4	3	5	5	5	3	4	73-**148**
Arjun Atwal	T95	Round 1	4	4	5	5	3	5	4	4	4	4	4	4	4	4	4	4	4	4	74
India	**T102**	Round 2	5	4	4	5	4	6	4	4	4	5	3	4	4	3	3	5	3	4	74-**148**
Tim Herron	T57	Round 1	4	4	4	4	2	5	4	3	4	4	6	4	5	4	4	5	3	3	72
USA	**T102**	Round 2	4	4	4	5	4	6	4	3	3	5	3	3	5	5	5	6	3	4	76-**148**

HOLE			1	2	3	4	5	6	7	8	9	10	11	12	13	14	15	16	17	18	
PAR	POSITION		4	4	4	5	3	5	4	3	4	4	4	4	4	3	4	5	3	4	TOTAL
Daniel Sugrue	T95	Round 1	4	4	4	5	3	5	3	3	4	4	6	4	5	3	4	5	4	4	74
Ireland	**T102**	Round 2	4	3	4	4	4	4	4	3	5	4	5	4	4	3	5	6	4	4	74 -148
Ben Willman	T57	Round 1	5	4	4	5	3	5	5	2	4	4	5	4	4	3	4	5	2	4	72
England	**T102**	Round 2	4	6	4	6	4	6	4	3	4	3	4	4	4	3	4	5	3	5	76 -148
Maarten Lafeber	T95	Round 1	4	4	4	5	4	6	4	3	3	4	4	4	4	4	4	4	4	5	74
Netherlands	**T102**	Round 2	6	4	4	5	3	4	4	4	4	4	5	4	5	3	3	5	3	4	74 -148
***Nick Flanagan**	T57	Round 1	3	4	6	4	3	5	4	3	4	4	4	4	4	3	5	5	3	4	72
Australia	**T102**	Round 2	3	4	4	5	4	7	4	3	4	4	4	4	4	3	6	5	4	4	76 -148
Sergio Garcia	T114	Round 1	4	4	4	6	3	5	4	4	4	4	4	5	5	4	4	5	2	4	75
Spain	**T102**	Round 2	4	4	5	5	3	5	3	3	4	4	4	5	3	3	5	4	3	6	73 -148
Aaron Baddeley	T95	Round 1	4	4	5	5	3	5	3	4	5	4	6	4	4	2	4	4	3	5	74
Australia	**T112**	Round 2	4	3	4	4	3	5	4	4	4	5	5	4	4	3	6	5	4	4	75 -149
Miles Tunnicliff	T95	Round 1	5	5	4	5	3	4	4	3	4	5	3	4	4	3	4	4	5	5	74
England	**T112**	Round 2	4	4	4	5	2	5	4	5	5	4	3	5	4	3	5	5	4	4	75 -149
Brian Davis	T57	Round 1	3	4	4	4	3	4	4	4	4	4	3	4	4	4	5	6	3	5	72
England	**T112**	Round 2	3	4	4	7	4	4	4	5	4	4	4	7	4	3	4	5	3	4	77 -149
Greg Norman	T73	Round 1	4	4	4	5	3	5	3	3	4	4	4	4	4	4	5	6	3	4	73
Australia	**T112**	Round 2	6	4	4	5	3	5	4	3	4	4	3	5	4	3	4	6	4	5	76 -149
Spike McRoy	T40	Round 1	3	4	4	5	3	5	4	2	4	3	4	4	5	3	6	4	4	4	71
USA	**T112**	Round 2	5	5	3	6	4	5	3	4	4	4	5	5	4	3	5	5	3	5	78 -149
Ben Curtis	T114	Round 1	3	4	4	5	5	4	4	4	4	5	4	4	4	3	5	6	3	4	75
USA	**T112**	Round 2	4	4	5	4	3	5	3	4	4	5	4	5	4	4	4	4	4	4	74 -149
Cameron Beckman	T114	Round 1	4	4	4	5	3	4	4	3	4	4	5	6	4	3	5	5	3	5	75
USA	**T112**	Round 2	4	4	5	4	2	5	4	3	4	5	4	6	4	4	5	4	3	4	74 -149
Zach Johnson	T73	Round 1	4	4	4	4	4	6	4	3	4	3	6	4	4	3	5	5	2	4	73
USA	**T112**	Round 2	4	4	5	5	4	5	5	3	3	4	4	4	5	3	5	4	4	5	76 -149
Stephen Ames	T95	Round 1	5	4	4	4	4	5	4	3	4	5	4	4	4	3	4	5	3	5	74
Canada	**T112**	Round 2	4	4	4	4	4	5	3	5	4	4	4	4	5	3	5	4	5	4	75 -149
Matthew Hazelden	T147	Round 1	4	4	3	5	4	5	5	3	5	3	7	5	4	4	6	4	3	5	79
England	**T121**	Round 2	4	4	5	5	4	5	4	4	4	3	3	4	4	3	4	4	3	4	71 -150
Anders Hansen	T128	Round 1	4	4	4	5	4	5	4	6	4	4	4	4	4	3	5	5	3	4	76
Denmark	**T121**	Round 2	5	4	4	4	3	6	4	3	4	5	5	4	3	3	4	6	3	4	74 -150
Simon Wakefield	T73	Round 1	4	4	4	4	4	5	4	3	4	4	5	5	4	3	4	5	3	4	73
England	**T121**	Round 2	4	4	4	5	3	6	3	4	5	4	4	5	4	4	5	5	4	4	77 -150
Richard Green	T95	Round 1	4	4	4	5	3	5	4	4	5	4	4	4	4	3	4	5	3	4	74
Australia	**T121**	Round 2	6	3	5	4	3	5	4	4	5	3	4	5	5	3	5	5	3	4	76 -150
Jonathan Kaye	T95	Round 1	4	4	4	4	5	4	4	2	7	5	4	4	4	3	4	5	3	4	74
USA	**T121**	Round 2	5	4	4	4	3	5	4	3	4	5	4	4	4	3	6	6	3	5	76 -150
Hidemasa Hoshino	T128	Round 1	4	3	5	5	4	5	5	2	4	4	4	4	4	5	6	5	3	4	76
Japan	**T121**	Round 2	4	3	5	5	3	6	4	2	4	4	4	5	4	3	4	5	4	5	74 -150
Simon Dyson	T114	Round 1	5	4	4	5	3	6	4	2	4	6	5	4	5	3	4	5	3	3	75
England	**T127**	Round 2	4	4	4	6	3	6	5	3	4	5	4	4	4	3	5	5	3	4	76 -151
Peter Hedblom	T142	Round 1	5	4	4	5	4	6	4	2	4	5	5	5	5	2	5	5	3	5	78
Sweden	**T127**	Round 2	4	4	4	4	3	6	4	3	4	4	6	4	5	3	4	4	4	3	73 -151
Tom Lehman	T73	Round 1	3	4	4	4	4	5	3	4	5	4	4	5	3	4	5	5	3	4	73
USA	**T127**	Round 2	5	4	3	6	3	5	5	3	4	4	8	4	5	3	4	5	3	4	78 -151

HOLE			1	2	3	4	5	6	7	8	9	10	11	12	13	14	15	16	17	18	
PAR	POSITION		4	4	4	5	3	5	4	3	4	4	4	4	4	3	4	5	3	4	TOTAL
Craig Perks	T95	Round 1	4	4	3	5	3	5	4	3	6	4	3	5	4	3	6	6	3	3	74
New Zealand	**T127**	Round 2	4	4	5	5	3	5	4	3	6	4	7	4	4	3	4	5	3	4	77 -**151**
Hennie Otto	T95	Round 1	4	5	6	5	2	5	4	3	5	4	3	6	4	3	3	5	3	4	74
South Africa	**T127**	Round 2	4	4	4	5	3	6	4	4	5	4	4	4	4	5	6	5	3	3	77 -**151**
Darren Fichardt	T40	Round 1	3	4	4	5	4	4	5	2	4	4	4	4	3	3	4	4	4	6	71
South Africa	**T127**	Round 2	4	4	4	6	4	5	4	2	6	5	6	6	5	3	5	4	3	4	80 -**151**
Eduardo Romero	T137	Round 1	4	5	5	5	4	6	4	3	5	5	4	4	4	2	5	5	3	4	77
Argentina	**T133**	Round 2	4	4	4	5	3	6	4	5	4	5	5	3	4	3	5	4	3	4	75 -**152**
***Brian McElhinney**	T128	Round 1	5	4	4	4	3	5	6	4	4	6	5	4	4	3	4	4	3	4	76
Ireland	**T133**	Round 2	4	4	4	4	3	6	3	3	5	4	5	6	4	3	6	5	4	3	76 -**152**
Scott Drummond	T73	Round 1	4	4	4	3	5	5	3	5	4	5	4	5	4	3	4	4	3	4	73
Scotland	**T133**	Round 2	5	4	4	5	3	5	4	5	5	5	4	4	6	3	5	5	3	4	79 -**152**
Graeme McDowell	T147	Round 1	5	4	4	6	3	5	5	4	5	5	4	6	4	3	4	5	4	3	79
N. Ireland	**T133**	Round 2	4	4	3	5	3	6	4	2	5	4	5	4	4	3	4	6	3	4	73 -**152**
Nick Faldo	T128	Round 1	4	3	5	5	3	6	4	3	4	4	4	5	4	5	3	4	4	6	76
England	**T137**	Round 2	5	4	4	4	2	6	5	3	4	4	6	3	4	4	7	4	3	5	77 -**153**
David Griffiths	T114	Round 1	4	4	4	5	4	8	4	3	4	5	4	4	3	3	4	4	4	4	75
England	**T137**	Round 2	5	6	4	6	3	5	4	4	4	5	5	4	4	3	4	5	3	4	78 -**153**
Thomas Bjorn	T95	Round 1	3	4	4	4	3	4	5	4	4	5	6	3	5	3	5	4	3	5	74
Denmark	**T137**	Round 2	6	7	4	5	4	4	4	3	4	4	4	5	4	3	4	4	3	7	79 -**153**
Jimmy Green	T142	Round 1	4	4	4	5	4	5	4	5	5	6	4	5	4	3	4	5	3	4	78
USA	**T137**	Round 2	3	4	5	4	3	5	5	3	5	4	6	5	5	2	4	4	4	4	75 -**153**
David Howell	T142	Round 1	4	5	4	5	4	5	3	4	4	6	4	5	5	4	3	5	4	4	78
England	**T141**	Round 2	4	4	4	5	3	6	4	3	4	5	7	4	4	4	4	4	3	4	76 -**154**
Nicolas Colsaerts	T137	Round 1	5	4	5	6	3	6	4	2	4	4	5	4	3	3	4	6	4	4	77
Belgium	**T141**	Round 2	4	4	5	5	2	6	3	3	5	4	6	5	5	4	4	5	3	4	77 -**154**
Frank Lickliter	T137	Round 1	5	3	4	5	4	5	3	3	5	4	4	4	4	4	4	6	4	6	77
USA	**T141**	Round 2	4	4	5	4	4	5	4	4	4	4	4	4	3	3	5	9	3	4	77 -**154**
Dinesh Chand	T152	Round 1	4	4	4	5	3	5	4	5	5	5	7	5	4	3	4	6	3	4	80
Fiji	**T141**	Round 2	4	4	4	5	3	5	5	2	4	5	4	4	5	4	4	5	3	4	74 -**154**
Paul Lawrie	T142	Round 1	4	4	4	5	4	5	4	3	6	5	4	6	5	3	5	5	3	3	78
Scotland	**145**	Round 2	4	5	4	5	4	6	4	3	5	4	4	4	4	3	5	5	3	5	77 -**155**
Louis Oosthuizen	T95	Round 1	5	4	4	4	5	4	3	4	5	4	4	4	2	4	4	4	4	5	74
South Africa	**T146**	Round 2	4	5	5	5	3	5	4	4	4	5	6	5	5	3	5	5	4	5	82 -**156**
Andrew Willey	T152	Round 1	3	4	5	5	4	6	4	3	5	4	4	4	6	4	6	5	3	5	80
England	**T146**	Round 2	5	4	6	4	4	5	4	3	5	4	5	5	4	3	4	5	3	3	76 -**156**
Ian Spencer	T147	Round 1	4	5	4	5	3	8	4	3	4	4	7	4	4	3	5	6	2	4	79
England	**T148**	Round 2	3	4	5	4	3	4	5	4	6	5	4	6	4	3	4	7	2	5	78 -**157**
Adam Le Vesconte	T137	Round 1	4	3	7	4	4	6	6	3	5	5	4	4	4	3	4	4	3	4	77
Australia	**T148**	Round 2	5	5	6	5	4	6	4	3	4	5	4	4	4	3	4	5	4	5	80 -**157**
Andrew Buckle	T128	Round 1	5	4	6	5	4	4	4	3	4	4	4	4	4	3	5	5	4	4	76
Australia	**150**	Round 2	4	5	4	5	3	8	3	3	5	6	5	6	4	3	7	4	3	4	82 -**158**
Yoshinobu Tsukada	T147	Round 1	4	3	6	5	4	5	4	3	5	6	6	4	4	3	4	6	3	4	79
Japan	**151**	Round 2	4	4	5	4	5	6	6	4	5	5	4	4	4	3	4	4	4	5	80 -**159**
Tom Weiskopf	T152	Round 1	8	4	4	6	4	5	6	3	5	4	4	5	4	3	4	5	2	4	80
USA	**152**	Round 2	6	6	4	4	3	5	4	3	6	7	4	5	3	3	4	5	4	4	80 -**160**

HOLE			1	2	3	4	5	6	7	8	9	10	11	12	13	14	15	16	17	18	
PAR	POSITION		4	4	4	5	3	5	4	3	4	4	4	4	4	3	4	5	3	4	TOTAL
Brett Taylor	156	Round 1	5	4	4	9	4	6	3	3	5	4	6	6	5	4	5	5	4	4	86
England	**153**	Round 2	4	4	4	6	2	6	4	2	5	5	5	4	4	4	4	6	3	3	75 -**161**
Neil Evans	155	Round 1	4	4	5	5	4	11	4	3	5	6	4	5	4	3	5	6	2	5	85
England	**154**	Round 2	4	6	4	4	4	6	5	2	3	5	6	4	4	3	4	6	3	5	78 -**163**
Lewis Atkinson	T147	Round 1	7	4	5	5	4	4	4	3	5	4	6	4	4	3	4	6	3	4	79
England	**T155**	Round 2	4	4	4	8	4	6	4	3	6	5	6	6	4	3	4	6	4	4	85 -**164**
Anthony Millar	T142	Round 1	4	5	3	5	3	5	4	3	4	5	7	5	4	3	4	5	4	5	78
England	**T155**	Round 2	5	4	5	5	4	6	4	4	6	4	5	8	4	4	4	6	4	4	86 -**164**

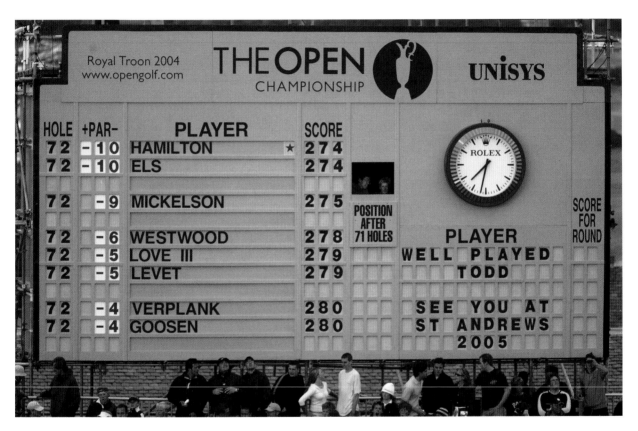

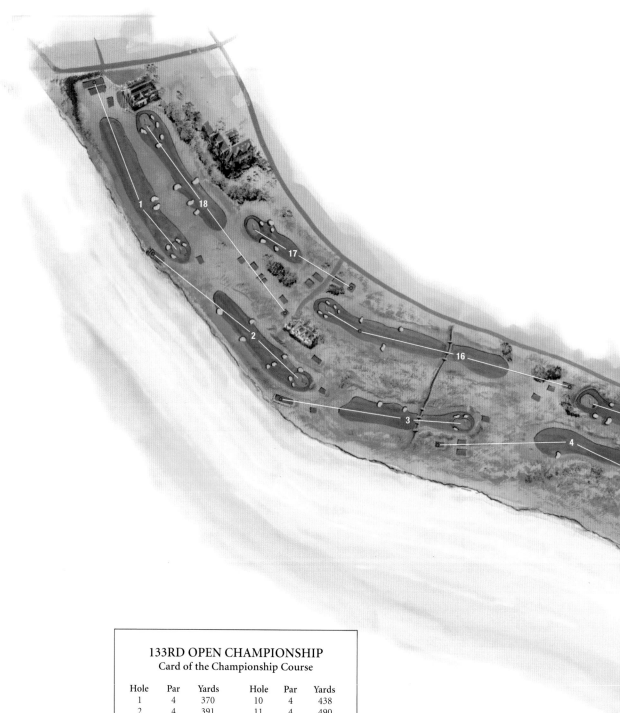

133RD OPEN CHAMPIONSHIP
Card of the Championship Course

Hole	Par	Yards	Hole	Par	Yards
1	4	370	10	4	438
2	4	391	11	4	490
3	4	379	12	4	431
4	5	560	13	4	472
5	3	210	14	3	178
6	5	601	15	4	483
7	4	405	16	5	542
8	3	123	17	3	222
9	4	423	18	4	457
Out	36	3,462	In	35	3,713
			Total	71	7,175